T0062962

The Life

of an

HVAC/R TECHNICIAN

John C. Schaub

 www.trafford.com
North America & international
toll-free: 1 888 232 4444 (USA & Canada)
fax: 812 355 4082

Dedications and Acknowledgments

This book has been dedicated to all the service technicians that have "been there" and can appreciate what it takes to work and excel in this field.

Grateful acknowledgment goes to my professional photographer son Rich Schaub, who without his vision and expertise would not have been able to capture my life's work in this cover. Thank you…love, Dad

I would like to thank the people at United Refrigeration for their loyalty and expertise over the last 45 years.

Thank you RSES for your 46 years of guidance

I would also like to lovingly thank my wife Joan of 50 years. Without her support and caring I would not have been able to keep John C. Schaub Inc. afloat for so many years.

Lastly I would like to thank my son Jack who is able to continue my legacy that I know will flourish for many years to come. You can find Jack and his flourishing business at www.chillers.com

COVER BY: SUPERIORIMAGESINC.COM

John C. Schaub

Contents

Dedications and Acknowledgements _____ 3

Introduction _____ 7

Chapter 1 Memories_____ **11**
Unique "On the job" stories

Chapter 2 Safety First_____ **21**
This is a guide for all technicians to avoid latent dangers on their daily tasks. This includes my own experiences, some both humorous and informative for their safety.

Chapter 3 Power Savings _____ **33**
This covers simple ways to save energy in millions of homes as well as in cold storage locker plants. This article was sent to President George W. Bush in 2001. I received a "thank you" from the White House, signed by President George W. Bush.

Chapter 4 Common Knowledge _____ **45**
Includes hard-to-find formulas and facts that may be used by technicians on a daily basis to resolve system problems.

Chapter 5 Troubleshooting _____ **65**
The correct approach to solving HVAC/R and chiller system problems. This also includes standard system start up techniques.

Chapter 6 Conversion Equations and References _____ **99**
A quick reference guide covering basic conversion equations applying to the HVAC/R industry. Electrical, temperature, and pressure references.

Bibliography _____ 101

John C. Schaub

Introduction

M y motivation to compose this book stems from the need to give the HVAC/R technicians a chance to live a fruitful and full life. Only those who have faced adversity on a daily basis would understand. I also wanted to pass on my wisdom to those people in homes throughout the USA who want to reduce their electric bills.

As a qualified technician, and exposed to thousands of HVAC installations over a sixty-year period, I will give you this valuable knowledge. I have met hundreds of HVAC/R technicians who stated they wished they had a reference book such as I have written. This is a "must read" book for the millions of technicians in the nation.

I have encountered the following experiences in over sixty years in the HVAC/R field, and they should bring memories of your own, similar to these. Some are humorous, while others seem unbelievable. I have dedicated this "telling all" book to the millions of HVAC/R technicians who have endured this "life style" and are proud of their accomplishments.

One of my most memorable was starting up 600 tons of air conditioning one hour before the 1953 "blackout" in New York City. I had taken the "tubes" to Jersey City before the lights went out. Is it possible I affected the lives of 8 million people? If so, I hope they accept my apologies for this indiscretion, since I added about two million watts to their already overloaded power lines.

John Schaub

John C. Schaub

THE LIFE OF AN HVAC/R TECHNICIAN

**Trouble shooting, Safety & Stories
dedicated to the
HVAC/R technicians**

John C. Schaub

Chapter 1

MEMORIES

In this industry, we have come a long way since they had belt driven compressors used in window units which weighted about 200 lbs. You hoped the windowsill was no higher than your elbows for obvious reasons. When started, two things would happen. First, the wall would shake and second, you had to raise your voice, because of the noise, to speak to the customer.

They sold thousands because at that time, in the late 40's, it was the only means of relief during hot weather. The only other solution was to buy a 10 lb. block of ice and use a fan. This "relief" lasted about two hours. If you had two strong arms and carried a ruler, (to measure the window), you were hired.

Decibel levels and BTU's were unknown. Only the British knew the latter unless you went to M.I.T. Your average wage was seventy-five cents per hour and didn't include compensation for mileage to the job site if you used your own car. Hard hats were usually the metal type (like in the first world war), and were discarded as soon as the foreman left the room. The technicians were aware of the dangers of quick <u>electrocution</u> with these hats on a hot day. (Salt and perspiration make a great conductor for electricity.)

Safety glasses were available, but were expensive..forget the side shields..they were not born yet. We were never asked to wear steel tipped shoes or non-skid soles on our shoes at this time.

DOUBLE TROUBLE

Working in a refrigeration manufacturing plant in Philadelphia one day in the late 40's I was wearing thin-soled sneakers. Guess what? While walking through the shipping department (lots of boards and nails), I stepped on a nail, which went clean through my foot and was protruding through the top of my sneaker. (It took a month to heal). Another "eye opener"-in the same plant, walking through the sheet metal shop, I felt a "ping" in my right eye while I was wearing safety glasses. I felt no pain and continued to work. However, the next morning when I awoke I was blind in my right eye. (I was already blind in my left eye from a childhood injury.) That morning a doctor removed a steel splinter from my right eye and saved my sight. The use of protective side shields in any area that may have flying objects is vital to anyone for eye protection. (Try to get in any E. I. Du Pont plant without them.)

ANOTHER CLOSE CALL

A similar occurrence happened on an army base in Dover, Delaware ten years later. We were starting a 100 HP direct drive compressor. It was only on a few minutes when I heard a loud noise, similar to shrapnel hitting metal. We immediately shut down the compressor. Under the direct drive coupling, we found a steel keyway, three times the size of a .45 bullet. Fortunately, the direct drive coupling had metal shields covering this area for just such a mishap.

In the 50's, it was common practice to use a chemical called carbon tetrachloride to clean compressor parts. This was done in a bucket usually in a closed room with no ventilation. The effect on a person's liver and lungs was devastating. It is wise, when using <u>any</u> cleaning agent, to have plenty of ventilation or to do this work outside the building. Along these lines, it is recommended you not smoke in an area saturated with CFC gases. It is known that when this gas is exposed to a flame, (including the halide torch), it will break down to a chemical similar to phosgene gas (similar to that used in the first world war). It's possible to lose your hair, organs, or worse if exposed too long to this toxic chemical. The smell alone of this gas, when passing through the element of a halide torch, will give you fair warning when you see the purple flame at the same time.

John C. Schaub

BOOM!

In the summer of 1967, I was called to service chiller units at a plastics plant near Flemington, NJ. I had finished my work and was in the office talking to the Plant Manager. Suddenly, a huge explosion shook the entire building. In the rear of this building were tanks containing a volatile liquid used in the production of plastics. A maintenance worker had opened a valve containing this liquid. Instead of closing the valve, he ran out of the building to save his own life. Seconds later, the liquid contacted a steam pipe which caused the tank to explode. I was told to run for my life because a second explosion was eminent. Instead, I ran toward the 200-foot high flames to get my truck and five thousand dollars worth of equipment. Without the truck and equipment, I was out of business. At the time, I did not realize the plant adjacent to this one was a high-octane gasoline refinery. If this had exploded, it would have created complete destruction within two miles of the blast. It's sad, but two men lost their lives instantly, and the man who opened the valve died in the hospital. Fortunately, the gasoline manufacturing plant did not sustain any damage. The lesson here is to know what you are doing or ask to be sure. What a costly mistake! The risks are high when working with pressurized systems, power, and fast moving objects, such as compressors, flywheels, and fans. If you are mentally incapacitated from alcohol, drugs, or even lack of sleep, stay away from any job that could lead to injury to you or someone else. Another condition is to be emotionally unstable. This could be caused by an argument, minor auto accident, and or any number of causes, which affects your ability to concentrate on the job at hand.

FROZEN STIFF

In the early 60's I was checking a low temperature chiller system (-20F.), which had lost several compressors at an army base in Virginia. I found what had happened. The compressor was overheating, causing the main bearings to seize. The problem involved the internal relief valve, which had a setting of 250 psig, between the high and low side of the compressor.

Due to the low temperature application, the differential pressure was 265 psig discharge, and 6 psig low side, equaling a 259 lb. differential pressure. Once a relief valve is opened, it may not reset due to the loss of spring tension or particles jammed under the valve seat. (A higher relief valve was installed.) Due to the equipment location, near high explosives, any work done required a fire truck and an ambulance standing by in the event of a fire. During the system check, a worker from the plant had opened a valve and was drenched with the –20F solution circulating the system. A low temperature liquid solution has about the same damaging effect to the tissues as heat does. It will cause third degree burns and requires immediate attention. Fortunately, the paramedics were there to administer instant aid and the damage to his skin was minimal.

ANOTHER WAY TO GET PAID

A refrigeration service company had not been paid for work done on a small refrigeration unit. Months went by and still no payment. The company knew if they removed the replacement parts they had installed, they would get nothing, and then the customer would call in another company. What they did was install a marble in the suction line. Every time the compressor came on, the marble was drawn toward the compressor suction port, closing off the gas flow. When the compressor shut off, the marble would roll down the suction line, the pressure would rise and the compressor would run. As we all know this is called "short cycling", with very little cooling done. After his customer had called in several other service companies without results, he paid his bill and was charged for the removal of the marble. (This is a true story and happened in New Jersey in 1940.)

BARREL OF HEARTS

I was involved on another job in a refrigerated area at a university hospital in Philadelphia. Among other items, it contained donated cadavers, which were hung by their ears in a manner similar to ice picks which carry blocks of ice. The medical students would remove a limb and dissect it in their classes. I was told that a technician had fallen into a barrel of hearts from a scaffold a few weeks earlier in the same room. What an experience! (I didn't want dinner that night!)

FROG'S LEGS

Another service call at a laboratory in Philadelphia involved 500 frogs, which had frozen because the liquid line solenoid valve (system on pump down) didn't close. We installed two liquid line solenoid valves in series and never lost another frog.

A PENTAGON SECRET

I had the opportunity to visit the Pentagon in Washington in the late 50's. They had lost eight compressors (10 HP hermetics) in one week on different units. All of the air-cooled condensers were on the roof with the compressors located in a package with the evaporator coils and air handlers. It was necessary to field pipe the discharge and liquid lines to each respective unit. These vertical lines averaged 15 feet in length, and were correctly sized and installed. It didn't take long to find the problem. At 10 AM each morning, the temperature adjacent to the condensers was over 100F due to the radiant heat absorbed by the roof. Secondly, the compressors would not start until about 10:30 AM or later. By this time, the liquid refrigerant from the condenser moved down the discharge line as a gaseous vapor and condensed as a liquid on the discharge side of the compressor. Even with a crankcase heater located on the suction side of the compressor, this would not prevent this refrigerant migration due to the mass of the compressor. The solution was to install a discharge line check valve adjacent in and on a horizontal line near the condenser to prevent this migration.

ELEVATION "DOES" MATTER

One job I visited in Baltimore, MD was typical of this situation. A water tower on a roof and located about 400 feet from the water cooled condenser, was tripping out on system high pressure safety on hot days. The air conditioning unit was never turned on until noon or later. Upon start up, the water in the tower reservoir was hot along with the pipes in the ceiling near the roof. This trip out could occur several times before the water was cool enough to have the system stay on line. This problem was solved by starting the pump and tower fan with a timer and cooling the water prior to compressor start up. This also prevented wear to the compressor.

ANOTHER TYPE PAD

Our race with the Russians to reach the moon first required many tests to insure the safety of the astronauts and the durability of the equipment. HVAC/R engineers and technicians were called upon to simulate the harsh conditions encountered in outer space. I was called to the GE Testing Center near Drexel University in Philadelphia to service a test chamber, which simulated cryogenic temperatures and absolute pressures approaching zero. This was in the late 50's, before we knew about weightlessness. This chamber simulated a rocket leaving earth and matched the temperature and absolute pressure as it climbed through the atmosphere. In this chamber were electronic parts, motors, and other components to test their durability. Now the reason I was called in you won't believe. A dryer had lost its desiccant and was circulating through the refrigeration system and someone had installed a cylinder containing Kotex pads to clean it up. What a mess! We had to disassemble the whole refrigeration system to clean it up, and this was the beginning of the age of technology!

NEEDED EAR PLUGS

Another thing you may not be aware of, during the cold war my company had received a contract from the U. S. Government to make portable units that made liquid oxygen in the field. This was a three-stage set up, using one compressor for the first stage, and the second compressor for stages two and three. Generators were used to power this system. The decibel level was so high you could hear this unit three miles away.

PRIMITIVE MEANS TO CHECK ABSOLUTE PRESSURES

Back in the 50's, a common practice in checking a vacuum was to use a thermometer with the bulb emerged in water. The thermometer was enclosed in a 3/4 inch diameter vial about 8 inches long. A 1/4 inch copper tube was inserted through a rubber plug with a flare nut attached to the other end to mount on the system being evacuated. The temperature – absolute pressure - was obtained in this manner. During that period, a 28.5" vacuum was considered satisfactory because of the single stage vacuum pumps used at the time. This equates to about 40,000 microns. (Ice would form on the outside of the vial at this absolute pressure.) Fifty years later, the multi-stage modern vacuum pumps can consistently drop the absolute pressure below 300 microns with electronic instruments to record this pressure. Isn't technology great! This is one of the reasons that the factory built refrigerators and freezers had such a great track record, relative to unit failures in the 90's.

WHAT EVER WORKS

During the end of the second world war, it was almost impossible to get compressor parts. On one job in Philadelphia, we had a valve plate crack along with the discharge reeds on a 50 HP belt driven compressor. A welder was called in to seal the valve plate crack, and we cut a tempered steel hacksaw blade to fit the size of the discharge reeds. This worked for one month until the correct parts could be obtained.

WORLD TRADE CENTER, NEW YORK CITY, 1972

The largest HVAC system I was on was also one of the tallest buildings in the world (at that time). Chiller units were placed every ten floors, which cooled ten floors below the chiller location. These units were lifted in place prior to the assembly of the building walls. (They weighed about 15 tons.) As you are aware, due to the elevation (over 1000 feet), the pressure at ground level would far exceed the maximum working pressure of any standard shell and tube vessel on the lower elevations. That's why they had separate systems every 10 floors.

BOAT WORKS – GROTON, CONN. (IN THE 60'S)

I was involved on the HVAC system (chilled water) for the first nuclear sub made in the USA. This system worked fine. However, prior to my arrival, for some reason, they could not properly run the nuclear system. They found out the pipes delivered to the job site were dropped on the ground and dirt had gotten into the ends of the pipes. I'm certain the HVAC/R technicians would not allow this to occur.

CHEWING GUM & ELECTRICAL TAPE

During my training years in the 40's, I was sent to service a cuber machine. I found a refrigerant leak on the discharge line near the compressor. I had come to the job site without a torch, solder, or vacuum pump. I decided to use chewing gum and electrical tape to seal the leak. With the line cold and pressurized to 10 psig, no bubbles showed. I proceeded to charge the unit. In leaving, I told the customer he would have ice cubes in about an hour. (I had the "duty" for that weekend and no one else was working.) On Monday morning, 40 guys knew what I had done, and I heard about it for ten years. I've remembered it for 53 years, and now all of you can tell me about it for another 50 years.

THE RATTAN CHAIR – 1945

I was sent on a service call to Ponzio's Diner near Camden, NJ. The customer placed the call because their humidifier wasn't working. In the back of the restaurant was living quarters for an elderly woman. After repairing the humidifier, I asked this sweet little old lady how she knew the humidifier wasn't working. "Easy" she said, pointing toward the rattan chair, "every time I sit in that chair it squeaks when the humidifier doesn't work."

THE FLYWHEEL – 1965 – NEW YORK CITY

A hotel was having repetitive breakage of a discharge line on one of two belt driven compressors adjacent to one another. An army of engineers from the plant, including me, visited the job site. At that time the "rule of thumb" was to balance a nickel on edge on the top of a compressor while running to determine the amount of vibration present. Well, with all the "experts" present, one engineer said "This is primitive and doesn't give the harmonics away from the source of the problem." The janitor, who was sweeping the floor tapped me on the shoulder and asked me, "why does that flywheel have buttons on it and the other one doesn't?" No buttons, no balancing. End of problem.

FINDING GOLD 1965 – PHILADELPHIA

I was working for Elliott Lewis Corporation at this time, and our service manager, John Dorfler, told me this story. One of our accounts called in the middle of July for service on his air conditioner. Upon arrival, the technician found the unit tripped out on high-pressure safety. It was found; a jewelry store had recently installed an exhaust fan with very hot air directed toward the water tower of this system. The metal parts of this tower were covered with gold! The jewelry store had been melting gold for whatever reason, and the fumes through the exhaust fan were depositing this gold by electrolysis on the water tower. I never heard what happened to this gold tower! (Of course, the hot air was diverted from the water tower.)

TELEPHONE COMPANY TRACING CENTER- TARRYTOWN, NJ -1961

As a field engineer for a leading manufacturer of compressors, I was requested to visit this job site due to repeated trip outs of the compressor circuit breakers. This compressor was a direct drive 75 HP unit used for air conditioning. By observing the oil in the crankcase bulls eye, I noted the color of the oil was black indicating moisture in the system. As you are aware, as the quantity of moisture increases in any refrigeration system, the oil break down temperature decreases to a point carbon begins to form within the circuit. This is due to the fact the discharge temperature exceeds the oil breakdown temperature limits. This affects the entire system due to sludge build up, reducing heat transfer, valves, refrigerant flow rates, compressor lubrication, and other nasty occurrences. Under certain conditions of percentages of air (oxygen), moisture, oil, pressures, and temperatures, a violent explosion can occur. I have actually witnessed flames through the compressor crankcase sight glass (the oil was burning) on one occasion. This is scary since you are helpless to abate the problem. Although this system was sick, it wasn't the entire reason for the compressor breaker trip outs. We removed the compressor heads and valve plates and found the problem. Someone had attached a ground connection to the copper water pipes to this system, causing an electrolysis effect, which coated the cylinder walls and other compressor internal parts with copper. The compressor motor was subjected to locked rotor conditions beyond its capabilities. It took a month to clean up this system, replace the compressor, and, of course, remove the ground wire. The copper pipes were insolated by using non-conductive rubber hoses (plastic pipe was not in general use at this time). The metallurgists said this would prevent the compressor copper plating, so they say.

Chapter 2

"SAFETY FIRST"

PIPING AND VIBRATION ELIMINATION

Any compressor, motor, pump, or engine will create vibration to some degree. The larger the mass and speed of these rotating objects, the greater the need to properly balance all internal parts. In the HVAC/R field, each installation presents its own problems since all piping is done on the job, as per specifications for that particular installation. On compressors operating with unloaders (capacity control), you have variable gas velocities through the system, which changes harmonics and pitch through the pipes.

I can, from my own experience, offer you suggestions to follow in this area:

1. On installing vibration eliminators on refrigeration discharge and suction lines, always install a pipe hanger support on the side away from the source of vibration. (This will help reduce vibration carry over to the pipe run.)

2. Any pipe run through a wall must have a sleeve (PVC or non corrosive material) around the pipe. This prevents corrosion from the chemical reaction caused by the building wall, (cinder block, concrete, etc.). It will also prevent damage to the pipe from vibration.

3. On horizontal water pipe runs, adequate pipe hangers must be installed, both for the weight and possible "whipping" action caused by the initial liquid flow upon pump start up. (There are charts available giving the number of hangers required depending on diameter, length,

---

and weight per foot.) If using PVC pipe, it is recommended schedule 80 be used for better support and possible "settling" between hangers.

4. Extra support must be considered when a pipe is at a height allowing a person to stand on the pipe.

5. Avoid running pipes near electrical equipment.

6. If you run pipe above walkways, keep them high enough to allow people, dollies, or tow motors to pass.

7. On a chiller system using one pump, it is important you maintain a proper GPM flow through the evaporator.

For example, if ten machines have chilled water delivered to these machines and only one is being used, with the others shut off, the flow rate will be too low at the evaporator tube bundle. Always install a ball check valve between the supply and return lines. Open this bypass valve enough to maintain adequate flow through the evaporator.

Under these conditions, the temperature difference through the low side evaporator should normally not exceed the delta "T" seen with all ten machines being supplied the chilled water. Each machine should be checked, (Delta T), and balanced for proper chiller water flow rate. It is possible the ball check bypass valve may have to be fully closed with all machines at full load. The readings on the temperature gauges will tell you what valves to open or close. The inlet valve on an unused machine should always be closed to prevent condensation from forming on the mold. As you change the percentage of machines used, it is important to check the temperatures to insure proper chilled water flow.

TECHNICIAN ETHICS

The HVAC/R field encompasses the world and beyond. We as technicians and engineers must follow the rules relative to safety, job performance, and efficient use of our time on every job.

The following list of things to do is for the service engineer:

1. On any service call, see the person who is responsible for maintaining

this HVAC/R equipment at the job site. If they are unavailable, speak to the person responsible for the system operation. By finding what happened prior to shut down or reason for non-performance, you can save a lot of time in diagnosis and correction.

2. If you find this problem occurred before, you may want to call the office for verification and what steps must be taken to correct the problem permanently.

3. Make a detailed report including pressures, temperatures, amperages, voltages, and anything that pertains to the problem.

4. The customer must always be treated with respect. Remember, they are momentarily upset because of the malfunction they believe is your company's fault. "Service call rage" serves no purpose.

5. Business owners and service managers-show respect to your workers. The worst thing you can do is to insult them in a crowd. This hurts! Call them aside and carefully explain, in a low voice, their good points and then any corrections they should make in their work habits. Remember, they are working somewhere away from you, and can cause havoc with your customers.

6. It is important, when working with your fellow worker, to try to share the workload equally for the benefit of all.

7. Hygiene - The work we do sometimes requires physical effort in high heat and humidity. At times, we must work in close proximity to another person. I often wonder how a person can start a day without a shower, body deodorant, or shoe powder. I hope the offenders read this article.

8. Try to minimize talking about your personal problems on the job. Too much of this could be distracting to fellow workers and appear to the customer as if your attention is not fully on their problem.

9. Be considerate to those near you. For example, don't place material in a walkway for others to trip over, or use a noisy drill when someone is talking on a phone, etc.

10. Remember, your appearance, language, personality, and knowledge goes a long way in telling others how nice a person you are.

THE DANGERS OF CHEMICALS AND GASES

Years ago, it was common practice to use carbon tetra chloride as a cleaning agent. This was used primarily for cleaning compressor parts during a rebuild. You would use an open tub filled with this liquid and clean the parts by using a wire brush. Most of the time, you were in an unventilated room and breathed the fumes from the tub for whatever length of time it took to do the job.

I usually left the room for a short period when my eyes became irritated and I couldn't stand the smell. It was later found this agent caused irreparable damage to the lungs and other bodily organs. The use of this cleaning agent has been banned for years.

The message here is to avoid any toxic substance which replaces air in its natural form in an enclosure.

Any time it is necessary to enter a room filled with refrigerant gas, it is common practice to use an oxygen mask. This is understandable since it would be possible to lose consciousness due to the lack of oxygen. The other reason could be more serious. If a fire or even an electrical short in the compressor has occurred, and the refrigerant gas has entered the area, you could be breathing phosgene gas, such as was used in the first world war. This is caused by the chemical breakdown of the refrigerant gas. Even when soldering a joint with refrigerant gas present, this deadly toxin will be produced. For the same reason, it is advised not to smoke in a room with refrigerant gas present.

MENTAL DISTRACTION

All of us have been faced with adversity, which temporarily has caused our minds to "lose" the thought process. An HVAC/R technician does not have the "luxury" to be distracted for one second. This can happen from an argument at home, someone cutting you off on the way to the job, and a thousand other reasons With luck and good judgment, you will live to my age.

LIGHTENING

Lightening is one of the most dangerous threats to injury and it strikes at 1/3rd the speed of light. Prior to a thunderstorm, lightening has been known to strike before the rain reaches the ground. Any work required, particularly involving roof top units should be stopped immediately until the thunderstorm is over. There are over 50,000,000 lightening strikes per year world wide, as reported by the U.S. Weather Bureau. Don't be a statistic!

LADDERS

The injuries sustained due to the improper use of ladders and scaffolds are endless. All ladder manufacturers must give the maximum weight allowed for that particular ladder and a warning not to stand on the top rung, which is printed on the ladder. This pertains to "A" ladders. The biggest mistake is using a ladder which is too short for the job. Understand, for stability, the rule of thumb is that the ladder must be placed at least three feet per ten feet of vertical rise from the building wall. Further, the base of the ladder must be level and on firm ground. Today, the use of aluminum ladders had reduced their weight per linear feet. However, two factors must be considered:

1. Since they are of light weight, the possibility on a windy day, for this ladder to fall is very likely.

2. The other danger is if the ladder touches a live electrical line, serious damage or injury can occur.

If either of these conditions were prevalent, it would be advised to secure the ladder with braces or rope for safety first. It is also advised to wear "nonskid" shoes and gloves for slippery rungs. The top of the ladder should be extended 4 feet above the roof level for ease of dismounting and mounting the ladder. Also stay in the center of the ladder to prevent the ladder from sliding due to unbalance.

SCAFFOLDS

Scaffolds are usually used by the duct and insulation technicians. A story I was told which occurred many years ago in Wilmington, Delaware involved five duct installers. A scaffold was placed on the side of a building about 50 feet from the ground. Due to the height, the installers were told to rope themselves to the scaffold. Four of the men did just that. Suddenly both supporting ropes holding the scaffold broke. Sadly, the only survivor was the unroped installer who jumped to safety. Upon investigation of the cause of the accident, it was found the total weight on the scaffold was beyond its capabilities. In this particular case, the scaffold was supported from the roof of the building since the work was done near this location. Other tragedies throughout the country have occurred on scaffolds erected from the ground due to overload and missing braces. If you have the occasion of working on these scaffolds, be certain they are erected properly and the supporting frame is within the prescribed weight limit.

ENCOUNTERS WITH THE UNKNOWN

It is common, in our daily work to inspect a building from top to bottom in order to properly size and install an air condition system. Some of the areas in the buildings we visit have not been seen for years, and as usual in an unused area, no lighting is available.

I was a project engineer in 1963 on the Dupont Playhouse job in Wilmington, Delaware, one of the oldest theaters in the country. On this job a light was on. The building was erected during the civil war and since steel was unavailable, the whole building was constructed with concrete. We were limited in the number of openings we could provide on the bearing walls, which would reduce the wall support when running the main air ducts from the air handler outside the building. After President Lincoln's assassination, all theaters in the nation sealed their private balcony boxes adjacent to the stage where Lincoln was shot, as this theater did in tribute to President Lincoln. It was necessary to open this area to run our ducts.

Believe it or not, we found one of Thomas Edison's original light bulbs still burning in this room! I guess the light bulb filaments were more durable in the 1860s, with DC current.

Unfortunately, two days later I was in the sub basement (without light) of this building and fell into a 3 1/2 foot round hole, 15 feet deep because my flashlight had low batteries and I didn't see the opening. It frightened the hell out of me, but by holding the sides with my feet and hands, I was uninjured. My hard hat, ear plugs, and safety glasses, which I wore, were still on after my descent. *The message here is to replace your flashlight batteries before they are too dim.*

THE CHOCOLATE FACTORY

In this field as a HVAC/R technician, your next service call could be anywhere in the industry. If you like variety, this type of work is for you. You must like noise, heat, cold, dirt, and difficult to reach unit locations. You are sometimes plagued with a service manager who is never satisfied and you meet some customers with explicit remarks like that heard in a football locker room.

My service call to a chocolate factory in New Jersey was different. The plant manager greeted me like a long lost brother. He stated that he couldn't go in the plant with me because he had more important things to do in his air-conditioned, clean, quiet office. He pointed to a maintenance man who was covered with chocolate dust and said, "he will show you the sick unit." I knew the cause of the "sick unit" before I left the office. This condensing unit looked like a very large chocolate nugget. Of course, the major problem was the unit location. Again, when arriving home, I had to remove my chocolate covered clothes before entering my home.

Advice: Carry a change of clothes for emergencies for all jobs.

THE "GLASS WOOL" EXPERIENCE

Back in the 40's and 50's this was the insulation primarily used in place of cork. It was lighter than cork and less expensive. I worked for Fogel Refrigerator Company in Philadelphia, PA, and they used this insulation in their display cases and walk-in boxes. I was given the job of unloading boxcars of glass wool on a railroad siding in the summer, in the sun. Due to the heat in the boxcar, (120 degrees) I decided to remove my clothing down to my pants, socks, and shoes. This was my first mistake. My second mistake was taking a cold shower immediately after finishing my work. On my way home I couldn't understand why I itched so much. I had a date that night, and wasn't going to cancel it. (At 18 years of age, who would?) This was my third mistake and almost cost me my forth-coming marriage. As you can surmise, I was covered with perspiration from head to toe. Any glass wool particles in the air would cling to a wet surface. Since I took a cold shower, my body pores closed leaving these particles protruding out like a miniature porcupine. The end of this story is a happy marriage and three boys to prove it.

Moral: Be protected from airborne particles for your health and romance.

TENNIS ANYONE?

Over the years I've cleaned, brazed, and assembled about three miles of copper pipe. After ten hours of this work one day, I received my reward. The doctor said I had tennis elbow. "Doc, I have never played tennis in my life" I said. I found any repetitive twisting motion of the elbow will cause damage and severe pain in this area. Matter of fact, he said, any joint in the body can be affected by a repetitive twisting motion in the same way. A shot of Cortisone (ouch) in the tender spot cleared it up in about a week. If I hadn't received the shot, he said it would have lasted for months. The doctor advised me to get a sedentary job. Who wants to work in an air conditioned quiet office?

In our daily work it is impossible to avoid hazardous and repetitive tasks. I believe taking a break now and then could actually speed up the completion of the installation, and save you from sore muscles.

OSHA (OCCUPATIONAL SAFETY & HEALTH ADMINISTRATION).

In 1970, President Richard M. Nixon signed the OSHA bill, which led to its creation in 1971. Since the start of this program, worker fatalities have dropped 50% and occupational injury and illness rates have declined by 40%. At present, OSHA has about 100 field agents to watch over 105 million workers at nearly 6.9 million sites. (That equates to 69,000 sites per field agent.) The HVAC/R field technicians and factory workers comprise about 1.5 million of this group. For example, there are at least 40,000 technicians in New York City alone. Our track record has been exemplary considering the type of work we do. With the odds being 69,000 to 1, a visit from an OSHA field agent is very remote. However, the OSHA rules are for your protection. As they say, "while the cat's away, the mice will play." Don't be a "statistic. Follow the rules and arrive home whole and healthy every day.

PRAISE FROM A SURGEON

During the late 50's we were installing an HVAC system for an operation room in a hospital in Camden, NJ. We were told a "patient required immediate surgery and time was of the essence to save his life". This was confirmed by the surgeon who walked into the compressor room to tell us the same thing. The amazing part was he stated, "How did you ever learn this complicated work?" I told him "the same way you learned your profession. By hard work, dedication, and the satisfaction derived from helping others over the years." Three hours later, the operation was a success and we were as proud as the surgeon! My "reward" was an emergency call on their blood bank four days later!

Note: All operation rooms today using explosive gases must have 100% outside air as opposed to recirculated air.

PROPER USE OF REFRIGERANT DRUMS

Years ago Dupont was the leading manufacturer of refrigerant. The trade name was "freon." Even today the age of a technician could be based on his use of this trademark on all refrigerants. In the past these drums were heavily walled. A 25 lb cylinder weighed about 10 lbs. empty and 35 lbs. full. The cost per pound was less expensive in the 125 lb. cylinders so many HVAC/R contractors would buy the larger cylinder and fill the smaller drums for convenience. Unfortunately, many of the smaller cylinders were overcharged, causing serious injury and damage. The wholesaler would give a rebate for any old cylinder return IF it didn't have burn marks on the drum. This practice is banned and heavy fines are imposed by the U.S. Government. Today, the refrigerant drums are light weight and the wholesaler charges you $5.00 to dispose of these containers.

A DUMB MOVE

A HVAC/R technician who had used a torch for years to remove refrigerant from a drum to hasten the charging process, decided to place the refrigerant drum in a kitchen oven since his normal (and illegal) method worked so well. A kitchen oven can reach a temperature of 500 degrees F. in short order, which would exceed the drum's pressure - temperature limits. Unfortunately the drum exploded while he was carrying it across the kitchen floor. He lived, but lost his leg in this accident. If he had only known a little warm water in a bucket would accomplish enough pressure rise in the drum to "chase" the refrigerant into the system he was trying to charge.

THE WOOLY HAT CAN SAVE YOUR LIFE

Early one morning on my way to an emergency call, I was driving down a side street in the center of Camden. I was in the middle of the block and gaining speed. Suddenly I saw a wooly hat, which was going between two parked cars toward the street. A little boy was on a bicycle heading into the street, directly in front of my car!!! I jammed on the brakes and stopped the car inches in front of the boy. Believe it or not, wearing that tasseled hat saved that boy's life. Always be alert in a congested area.

HOSPITAL DELIVERY ROOM-THE NEED FOR EAR PLUGS

I had the pleasure of being asked to service an air conditioning unit at West Jersey Hospital in Camden, NJ in the 50's. At that time, ear plugs were not mandatory and very few HVAC/R technicians used them for high decibel areas. God choose the right gender to deliver these little cherubs, because I truly believe our role was far less painful. The noise level was equal to an Army - Navy game in Philadelphia! My repair of the air conditioning unit did help. God bless my mother and all the mothers in the world.

ADVICE FROM A MATURE HVAC/R TECHNICIAN

If you like diversity, daily challenges and the desire to excel in this field, your rewards will be limitless. Today, the need for HVAC/R technicians with knowledge and experience is very important. The manufacturers, engineers, and designers of HVAC/R equipment have used their skills to develop the most modern type units in the world. It has improved our living conditions beyond all expectations. However, without proper installation, start up, and maintenance by dedicated HVAC/R technicians, very few systems will endure the test of time.

John C. Schaub

Chapter 3

POWER SAVINGS

Below are lists of household items that can be checked to save energy and, ultimately, your money.

1. **Oil, gas or hot water heater**

   A. Reduce temperature setting to 125 - 130 F.

   B. Install time clock. Suggested setting: (Off 9:00 p.m.-On 5:00 a.m.)

   C. Insulated hot water heater.

   D. Flush hot water heater reservoir at least yearly.

   E. Check local library for solar heat systems.

2. **Fireplace chimney seal**

   The loss of heated air is considerable, which also creates a negative pressure in the house or building allowing cold air to enter in many locations. A chimney seal can easily be installed and removed in the event you use your fireplace. Check in the phone directory for a fireplace outlet in your area.

3. **Refrigerator**

   A. Clean the back and underside of the refrigerator once a year. Vacuum or blow through.

   B: Check door gaskets with a strip of newspaper- see if there are any gaps

   C: Do not overfill. this will cause poor air circulation and subsequent food loss.

D: Using a thermometer, check the temperature in the refrigerator (36-40F) and freezer (0-10F)

E: Do not place refrigerator next to a heat source or location with poor air flow.

Notes: The higher the freezer temperature, the faster bacteria growth will form when food is left in the freezer for long periods. Place a thermometer in each area and wait 20 minutes. Check the temperatures. If the temperatures are lower or higher than the normal range (listed above) then adjust the "cold" knob in each area. Check again in twenty minutes.

4. Christmas and holiday lights

Years ago, 120 volt light bulbs were used - if one went out, they all went out on that string. The expense of using these bulbs was very costly. I recommend using the "peanut bulbs" or a voltage step down transformer type with a low voltage string; they are far more cost effective.

5. Lights in the home or office

Cutting your utility bill can be as simple as replacing your conventional bulbs to compact fluorescent bulbs, which use much less energy and last about 10 times longer.

Example: One 100 watt conventional bulb will cost .15 cents/day average if on for 10 hours. Most hardware stores carry these long life bulbs. This is based on a $.15 cost per kilowatt-hour.

Install a timer: A great loss of energy is forgetting to shut off those holiday lights and finding that only the owls enjoyed the view. Installing a $5.00 timer will help reduce your electrical bill and the hassle of shutting off the lights.

6. Outside lights

Most homes have outside spotlights. One 150-watt incandescent bulb will cost you 20 cents average, per night, depending on your kilowatt cost. By installing motion sensors, the light will operate only when someone crosses the sensor. Most can be set from 2 to 15 minutes. They may be obtained from your local hardware store. It may be wise to contact a certified electrician for this work.

Note: You will pay for the motion sensors in a year or less.

7. **Dryer vent**

Most dryers have an air vent, which in time will block the outdoor vent from lint build-up. This can cause overheat and nuisance trip-outs of high temperature safety, or worse. Clean the outlet vent thoroughly. This will also allow the flap to close properly to prevent cold air from entering the building. This will shorten dryer cycle time and save power. Also check the flexible duct from the dryer to the outside air vent for any leaks or crimps.

8. **Outside air openings**

Most buildings have the water pipes located on the outside wall. Check these pipes for openings around the pipes - seal all openings to prevent cold air and insects from gaining entry. Use steel wool or spackle the openings. Also seal electrical outlets located on an outside wall with plugs.

9. **Building insulation**

Well insulated homes are the most comfortable; winter and summer. The "R" factor will determine the loss of heat, along with the thickness of the insulating material. Many types of insulation are on the market today, which were unavailable 20 years ago. The older the insulation the more likely the "R" factor will be far below what will give you a satisfactory comfort zone for your home. Also, the older types of insulation tended to fall apart due to moisture accumulation and rotting over the years. A simple test can be done by feeling the walls on the inside of your home or office. Make sure that the wall is an outside wall and the outside temperatures are cold. The next step would be to call a local insulating contractor to check the actual temperatures and give you a price on re-insulating your home.

In most cases, what they would do is blow insulation into your walls between the joists. Most contractors guarantee would be 10 or more years.

Depending on the heat loss, without this work, you may recover your cost in as little as three years. Your fuel and electric costs would be reduced by 30% and you would have a comfortable home in the mean time.

10. Thermal paint and roof color

A new type of paint made by DuPont, which comes in light colors, will reduce the heat flow considerably. This paint does not crack or peel if properly applied. You should be able to find a contractor locally who would guarantee good results. If you are contemplating a new roof, pick a light color. Darker colors add to the heat in your attic.

11. Trees and shrubs

The use of shrubs along the outer periphery of your home will reduce heat loss or gain. Shade trees, in time, will reduce heat gain considerably.

12. Heating unit

A.   Air filters:

The most important item in your HVAC system to be checked is the air filters. With clogged filters, the air flow is reduced to a point where the unit will run continuously and not cool or heat your building. You are using fuel and power far beyond the need.

NOTE: Change air filters once a season

B.   Fan control:

Setting the delay fan control, if adjustable, at 85F off and 125F on will maximize your heat potential. You will get heat sooner and prevent the non production effect by no air flow.

C.   Blower fan wheel:

Dirt accumulating on the fan wheel blades will cause a reduction in air flow. Before checking, shut off power to Unit. If dirty, clean each vane, which will increase the air flow.

D.   Fan Belt:

Units with fan belts (as opposed to direct drive) require inspection. These belts dry out or stretch, causing slippage. Replace a belt, which is worn or loose. Make sure it is the same size. Belt tension can be adjusted so it's not too tight or too loose.

NOTE: Belt slippage can be heard at start up of the fan.

E. Thermal Pane Windows:

Twenty five percent of your heat is lost through single pane windows. (Based on a 0F outside, 70F inside). Use of thermal windows will allow a higher moisture content when using a humidifier, giving more comfort at a lower indoor temperature setting.

F. Thermostat:

Install a time clock or manually lower thermostat a few degrees. this will save you 5-10% on fuel and power costs.

G. Humidifier:

During the winter months, the moisture content in the air indoors is directly affected by the outside temperature. The lower the temperature, the less moisture can be held indoors which causes dry skin, static electricity and uncomfortable living conditions.

Installing a quality humidifier can substantially reduce these problems. The thermostat can be lowered giving you a savings of fuel and power usage.

These humidifiers are available in any air conditioning supply house with instructions for installation. OR, you can call a heating company and have them install this unit complete with power wiring and piping, which I suggest.

13. **Cooling unit**

A. **Crank Case heater:** At the end of the cooling season, shut off the breaker to the outside condensing unit.

NOTE: This does not apply to heat pumps.

REASON: Most compressors are equipped with a heater to prevent liquid refrigerant build-up during the off cycle, which would damage the compressor. These heaters can use up to 100 watts of power and are useless during the winter months.

SOLUTION: Shut off breaker or remove the fuses to the outdoor condensing unit.

CAUTION: Turn on this breaker or replace the fuses 24 hours prior to unit start up. You can expect a savings from 30-40 dollars during the winter months.

B. **Outside Condensing Unit:** In the Spring, remove the top grill and clean out any debris in the bottom of the unit carefully. Again, shut off the power when working on the unit. Do not cover the entire unit during the winter months.

REASON: Moisture forms on the controls causing shorts (a cover on top of the unit is fine)

Make sure the unit is level for efficiency.

C. Evaporator (Cooling Coil):

This coil is located adjacent to the air handler and accumulates air-borne dirt due to the wet surface and the close proximity of the fins. Check for cleanliness. Poor air flow equals poor unit performance. Call in a HVAC company for inspection if necessary.

D. By-Passed Air:

All air must go through the cooling coil. Check around unit for any air loss and seal with duct tape.

14. **Safety**

A. **Smoke Detectors:** Should be located in bedrooms, garage, workshop, laundry room. Have one on every level. Most new construction homes ask that a smoke detector be in every bedroom and on every level. Check with your local codes. A remote smoke detector can be placed above a Christmas tree on the wall or ceiling.

B. **Fire Extinguishers:** Place one near your heater, kitchen and workshop.

C. **Carbon Monoxide Detectors:** This is a must when using gas for heating or cooking. Since the gas is odorless, you have no warning of its deadly presence.

John C. Schaub

D. **Lightning Rods:** It has been estimated that 20,000,000 lightening strikes occur yearly. The power per strike is 2,000,000 volts. The temperature is 55,000 degrees F. This is world wide. It is recommended that lightning rods be installed on your home or building to eliminate possible entry of this awesome power into the home or building. Do not take a shower or use the phone during an electrical storm!

E. **Gasoline Fumes:** Never allow gasoline fumes to enter the area near your heater.

15. Generators

In the event of a power outage, an alternate source of power should be available. The generators manufactured today are state of the art machines with 99% reliability. Included in some power packages is an "auto start." Loss of power will automatically switch your power source in seconds and run until the primary power is restored.

At this point, the generator is shut down automatically and switched to the primary power source. As usual, the power loss occurs during violent weather conditions and could last for days or even weeks.

16. Roof fans

It is advised that a roof fan be installed to remove the super heated air from the roof crawl space area during the hot summer months. The fans come equipped with a built in thermostat and will only let the fan run when the air exceeds what ever temperature you set it (90F is a good setting). You will also require a ventilator opening at either end of your home or office. This may already be built into your building.

It is also advised to use 15 inches of insulation (see insulation section for more), between the top floor ceiling and the crawl space. The reason a top floor is more difficult to cool is because your ceiling on the top floor is a huge radiant heat panel even after the sun goes down.

Benefit: Cooler Bedrooms and lower electric bills.

17. Transformer type power packs

Many homes are equipped with power pack devices. They include: chairs with vibrators, electronic games, dust busters, train sets, baby monitors, battery re-chargers and cell phones. Unplug these items when not in use for long periods.

18. House exterior color

One of the largest energy uses in your home or office is the central air-conditioning system. Two ways to reduce your energy cost would be:

A. Have a light colored roof and siding.

B. Provide shade trees, particularly on the west and south sides of the dwelling. If your home has not been constructed yet, consider the least amount of windows facing north.

19. Location of air-conditioning unit

If possible, the outdoor condensing unit should be placed on the east side of the home to prevent the direct rays of the sun hitting the unit during the afternoon. The sun can heat up the surface of the coils making the unit less efficient. The idea here is to put the unit in the shade to increase the unit's efficiency.

20. Well pumps

If you have a well, check the pump to see how long it takes for the pump to turn on after water is turned on. It should take, on average, 1 minute or more. If not, either your reservoir tank has no air cushion or your pressure switch is improperly set. This condition will increase your electric bill causing greater wear on the pump and motor.

21. Dish Washers

Try and completely fill the dishwasher for economy. All dishwashers have heating coils, pump sprayers, and dryer fans. They use a considerable amount of power. They are listed 3rd in the average home for power usage.

THE LIFE OF AN HVAC/R TECHNICIAN

22. Electric range

The highest for power consumption, in the average home, is the electric range. It's common to leave the range on after you have cooked your food. Please save your money and turn it off. If you heat with gas, you may consider a gas range if you use your electric range frequently.

Your overall savings will be about 30%.

23. Vacation homes

If you plan to visit a vacation home during the off seasons, shutting off the electric, gas and water and draining the pipes would be impractical. However, other steps should be taken for power savings:

A. If leaving for the season, turn thermostats to 55F in the winter and the cooling "off" in the summer.

B. Shut off the refrigerator. (Please remove the food first)

C. Turn off the clocks, TV and VCR (anything that uses power)

D. As at home, turn off power to the outside condensing unit because of the crank case heater located in the cooling unit section.

Open doors under the kitchen and bedroom sinks, if they are located next to an outside wall. With the house temperatures set at 55F, it is possible the pipes may freeze at these locations if the cold air can get into those places.

24. Miscellaneous

Close doors and supply air outlets in rooms that are not being used often. Examples would be the extra bathrooms not used, laundry rooms that are normally warm already and the large walk in closets.

Learn to turn off lights as you move room to room and any other appliance including the television when not in use.

25. Energy saving for cold storage plants

My many years of trouble shooting in the HVAC/R field have led me to share my knowledge relative to energy conservation in cold storage plants.

John C. Schaub   41

Our nation is facing an energy crisis due to inadequate power plants. With an estimated 100,000 cold storage plants here and abroad, much can be done to lower their power usage.

With the "state of the art" technology now available, many companies have upgraded their refrigeration systems for better product preservation and economy. However, 80% of the existing cold storage plants were installed twenty or more years ago, and may need some simple guidance, which does not require complete removal of the present system.

A. Superheat:

A system tonnage is based upon the pounds of refrigerant circulated per minute through the evaporator. For convenience, most technicians will take this reading on the suction line near the compressor. This reading should be taken on the suction line near the bulb, which controls the refrigerant flow when using a thermal expansion valve. When having multiple evaporators, it is imperative this be done. Also, the reading should be taken on the side of the suction line, not at the top or bottom because the readings will be false. The TX valve bulb should also be placed on the side of the suction line for the same reason. The bulb straps must be tight for good heat conduction. Most TX valve manufacturers pre-set their valves at 10 degrees F. I prefer 8 degrees F. to allow more refrigerant in a liquid state in the evaporator. This will increase the tonnage and reduce the compression ratio since you will be running a higher suction pressure.

B. Compressor Operation: - (Air Cooled Condenser)

Most compressors are located on the building roof with the condensing unit. During the summer months, the ambient temperature can exceed 120 degrees F. during the day at this location. Depending upon the operational temperature in the storage area, the compressor performance could drop to 50% output. This equates to about twice the energy use per BTU displaced. The other factor is compressor body temperature. As the discharge pressure increases so does the temperature. The compressor oil viscosity is reduced effecting compressor lubrication. Also, refrigeration oil has a break down temperature which must be considered in low temperature, high compression ratio operation. To save energy and to give the compressor a "cool down" period, it is advised it be shut down in fifteen minute increments per hour during high outside ambient conditions. This would apply for "holding rooms" only.

C. **Power Demands:**

Most power companies charge for "spikes" in the morning and evening hours during high power usage. Since a compressor, upon start-up, will draw 4 to 5 times the normal "run" current, it is important to minimize compressor start-ups at this time. Please call your power company for these hours.

D. **Evaporator Fans In Cold Storage Holding Rooms:**

For rapid heat transfer, air is driven through the evaporator by the fan, which in turn cools the product in the cold storage room *while the compressor is running*. When the compressor is off, no heat transfer takes place. As a matter of fact, the evaporator fan motor *adds* heat to the room. Still air in a cold storage room also acts as a barrier on the walls to reduce heat from entering the room. To save energy and reduce heat transfer, it is recommended the evaporator fans be shut off with the compressor.

E. Un-trapped drain lines can become another source of heat gain to the evaporator. Since a slightly negative pressure is created by the fan, air from outside is drawn up the drainpipe and into the storage room. I would also advise checking the outside walls for other sources of air loss or gain such as around pipes or steel supports entering the storage room.

In summation, keep your system clean, motors lubricated, and do not get locked in the cold storage room.

Chapter 4

"COMMON KNOWLEDGE"

REFRIGERATION BASICS FOR ENGINEERS AND TECHNICIANS

The following article is one I wrote, as a sixty year veteran in the chiller service industry. This is the most comprehensive article covering everything from superheat and subcooling to thermal valves and capillary tubes. It also explains everything from ohms law to BTU's. The following sections will show key notes examples and equations.

REFRIGERATION:

KEY NOTES AND EXAMPLES:

- Defined as the removal of heat. It may also be described as the transfer of heat by a mechanical means from one object or space to another.

- Heat is energy. Something that can be neither created nor destroyed. It cannot be seen.

- Heat and temperature - concentration of heat - example: lighted candle

- Cold - Lack of heat (consider heat as a substance) example: 2 gallons of water - spread out at lower temperature

- Temperature - expression of the concentration of heat in a substance. Example: 1 lb. of water at 100F = 100 B.T.U.'s and 10 lb of water at 10F = 100 B.T.U.'s

---

- Sensible heat: Heat that can be felt

- Temperature Scales: 2 types - Centigrade and Fahrenheit.

- B.T.U. = British Thermal Unit (Heat required to raise 1 lb. of water 1 degree Fahrenheit)

- 1 Calorie = 1 gram of water raised from 0 C to 1 C (centigrade)

- Rapidity of heat flow depends upon temperature difference.

- Common known BTU values: 144 B.T.U.'s (latent heat) required to change 1 lb. of water to 1 lb. of ice. 970.4 B.T.U.'s (latent heat) required to change 1 lb of water to 1 lb of steam.

- Sublimation: Change of a solid to a gas.

- Regulation: Change of a gas to a solid.

- Heat capacity may be defined as: the amount of heat required to raise the temperature of 1 lb. of substance 1 degree F (Fahrenheit)

- Capacity = Ability of substance to absorb (give up) heat.

- In order of heat capacity (least to most)-1. Aluminum, 2. Iron, 3.Copper, 4. Zinc, 5. Lead

- Heat capacity of water is 1 (Specific heat is the same thing) Example: Specific heat of water is 1.00, while the specific heat of iron is only .113…almost 9 times less than water.

- Specific heat of ice is .5

EQUATIONS:

- B.T.U.'s = weight X specific heat X temperature difference. (W. x S.H. x T.D).

HEAT TRANSFER:

Key notes and examples relating to heat transfer:

- **Radiation:** Heat transfer that travels in straight lines. Example: The sun.

- **Conduction:** Heat transfer that travels by contact of molecules.

- **Convection:** Heat transfer through a 3rd medium. Example: Air

- **Sensible heat:** Heat that can be felt.

- **Specific heat (SH):** Heat per unit of mass required to produce a degree rise in (F)

- **Latent heat: (LH)** Change in state without a change in temperature.

- **Temperature difference (TD)**

- **Refrigerant Effect (RE)** = Heat Content Vapor - Heat Content Liquid (R.E. = HCV – HCL)

- **A refrigeration system is more effective with a higher back pressure.**

EQUATIONS & EXAMPLE PROBLEMS RELATING TO HEAT TRANSFER:

PROBLEM #1 How many B.T.U.'s required to raise temp. of 10 lb. water from 0F to 212F (steam)?

- B.T.U.'s = from 0F to 32F (ice) = W. x S.H x T.D. (10 x .5 x 32)=160 B.T.U.'s

- B.T.U.'s = from 32F ice to 32F water = w. x 1.h. (10 x 144) =1440 B.T.U.'s

- B.T.U.'s = from 32F water to 212F water = W. x S.H. x T.D. (10 x 1 x 180) =1800 B.T.U.'s

- B.T.U.'s = from 212F water to 212F steam = W. x L.H. (10 x 970.4) = 9704 B.T.U.'s

Total No. B.T.U.'s   13,104

PROBLEM #2 How many tons refrigeration required to reverse this process in one minute?

- 200 B.T.U.'s per minute per ton (standard equation)

SOLUTION: 200/13,104 = **65.52 tons**

PROBLEM #3 How many B.T.U.'s required to lower temp. of 500 lb fresh beef from 80F to -5F?

- Specific heat of beef before freezing .650
- Specific heat of beef after freezing .369
- Latent heat of fusion 81 B.T.U.'s per lb.

Solution:

- Weight x Specific Heat x Temp. diff. or W. x S.H. x T.D.
- 500 x .650 x 48 from 80F to 32F = **15,600 B.T.U.'s**
- Weight x Latent Heat or W. x l.h.
- 500 x 81 from a liquid to solid = **40,500 B.T.U's**
- Weight x Specific Heat x Temp. Diff. or W. x S.H. x T.D.
- W. x S.H. x T.D. (500 x .369 x 37) = **6,826.5 B.T.U's**

TOTAL B.T.U.'s required = 62,926.5

PROBLEM #4 What is the refrigerant effect produced by 1 lb. R-12 with a condensing temp. of 90F and a back pressure of 30 lb.?

- 90F Condensing Temp. (HCL)= 28.70 B.T.U.'s
- 30# back pressure (HCV)= 81.83 B.T.U.'s
- R.E. = HCV – HCL
- R.E. = 81.83 - 28.70 = **59.58 B.T.U.'s per lb.**
- Condenser ton = 250 B.T.U.'s per minute and Evaporator ton = 200 B.T.U.'s per minute
- lbs. refrigerant per minute is (200 x (tons load)) /refrigerant effect

PROBLEM #5: How many pounds of refrigerant needed per minute in a 5-ton system if the discharge pressure is 161.5 lb, and the suction pressure is 17.10 lb.?

- R.E. = HCV – HCL
- R.E. = 79.82 - 36.66 = 43.16
- (200 x (tons load)) / R.E=(200 x 5) / 43.16 =

Solution: 23.16 lb. of R-12 needed per minute

KEY NOTES AND EXAMPLES RELATING TO STATES OF MATTER

- **Solids:** Definite volume and shape. Example: baseball.
- **Liquids:** Definite volume but takes shape of container. Example: water in a glass
- **Gases:** Have neither definite volume nor shape. They not only take shape of container but they expand and fill it. Example: air in a balloon
- The addition of heat to a substance that exits as a solid will transform that solid to a liquid and continued addition of heat will change it from a liquid to a gas. In addition, heat will expand solids, liquids, and gases.
- Ammonia will solidify at -108 F. at 14.7 atmospheres
- R-12 will solidify at -247 F at 14.7 atmospheres
- When physical heat is added to a substance without a change in temperature, it is called latent heat.
- Latent heat of evaporation is an example of liquid to gas
- Latent heat of condensation is an example of a gas to a liquid.
- To change 1 lb. of water from 212 F water to 212 F steam requires 970.4 B.T.U.'s
- Latent heat of Fusion: Water to Ice - 144 B.T.U.'s per pound
- Sensible heat: Heat that can be felt. (Increase or decrease of temp. in a substance without a change of state.)

- Water reaches its greatest density at 39.2 F. This is why it freezes on the surface of any body of water.

- **Total Heat:** Sum of sensible and latent heat.

- Heat will flow from a warmer to a colder substance

- **Pressure:** Atmospheric pressure 14.7# ABS (Reckoned from a weight of a 1 sq. inch column of air starting at sea level and extending upward 100 miles.)

- As the pressure decreases, the boiling point also decreases.

- At double atmosphere, (approx. 30 lb.), water boils at 249 F.

KEY NOTES AND GUIDELINES REGARDING REFRIGERATION

- Saturated gas means wet gas.

- Saturation point is when wet gas becomes 100% vapor

- Superheat is sensible heat.

- At expansion valve approximately 90% by volume is flash gas.

- Ratio of Compression: Ration of absolute pressures before and after compression

- Ratio of Compression Formula: (Head pressure + 14.7)/ (Back Pressure + 14.7)

- VW compressors, when operating on 25% capacity, will use only 28% of total current output at full load.

- R-12 refrigerant boils at -21.6 F - absorbs its latent heat of evaporation.

- R-12 solidifies at -252 F

- R-11 boils at 74.7F and solidifies at -168F

- R-22 boils at -44.14F and solidifies at -256F

- Methyl Chloride boils at -10.6F and solidifies at -144F

- Ammonia boils at -28F and solidifies at -107F
- Adjustable thermal valves:
  - Sporlan thermal valve will rise or fall 2 F for every ½ turn "P" valve.
  - Sporlan thermal valve will rise or fall 4 F for every ½ turn "O" valve.
  - Alco thermal valve will rise or fall 2 F for every full turn (standard cage).
  - Detroit lubricator will rise or fall 4 F for every full turn.

EQUATIONS AND EXAMPLE PROBLEMS:

PROBLEM #6 How do you calculate the CFM and lb. or air which must be delivered by the evaporator on an air conditioner per ton of lead for a given range?

- lb./min/ton = 200/(Range x .24)
- 4 x 4 compressor = 1st figure is cylinder bore. (in inches)
- 2nd figure is length of stroke (in inches)
- **In computing the cubic feet per minute of refrigerant circulated within a system the following formula is used:**

CFM = ((Pi R) x 2) x H x R.P.M. x No Cyl. x .75)/1728

Example: 4 x 4 ammonia compressor. With 800 R.P.M.'s, how many cubic feet per minute of refrigerant circulated?

Answer: (3.1416 x 4 x 4 800 x 2 x .75)/1728 = 34.9 cubic feet. This is the amount of gas compressor will handle. Velocity Ft./min = (No. lbs. refrigerant circulated x Sp. Vol.)/(cross sectional area of suction line in sq. ft.)

PROBLEM #7 What is the gas velocity (in ft. per min.) of a unit handling 24 lbs R-12 per min. with a 2-1/8: o.d. suction line? (28.4 lbs back pressure = Sp. Vol. of .939)

Answer: (24 x .939)/.025 sq. ft. = 1046.72 ft. per min.

- d x d x 7854 will also give the area of a circle.

- Minimum requirement for R-12: 100 ft./min.

- **Note:** On the above problem, the specific volume is taken from the chart in the York Service Manual.

PROBLEM #8 A refrigerant chiller system has an 8 ton load and uses 16 gallons of water per minute. The temperature of the water (load off) is 67 F. What should be the temperature of the water with (load on)?

- Tons = (GPM x range)/30

- 8 = ((16 x (? - 67)) / 30

- Therefore : 16 = (30 x 8 tons)/range = 15

Answer: 82 F (With the water temperature with the load off is 67 F, an increase (load on) of 15 F will give you 82 F.)

Note: G.P.M.'s and tons could be computed in the same manner.

NOTES:

- The figure 30 in the above formula is an abstract number obtained by dividing 8.3 (the weight of 1 gallon of water) into 250 (the number of B.T.U.'s in one condenser ton). When using the number 30, it is unnecessary to change gallons of water to lbs. of water, thereby simplifying the formula.

- Also when figuring evaporator tons, the number 24 will be used in the place of 30. The reason being 8.3 is divided into 200 (This is the number of B.T.U.'s in one evaporator ton.) It is more commonly known as gallon degrees.

KEY NOTES & GUIDELINES REGARDING
ELECTRICAL APPLICATIONS

- Ohms Law = E / (I x R)
  - E = Volts

- I = Amperes
- R = Resistance
- E x I = Watts
- 746 watts = 1 h.p.
- Kilowatt = 1000 watts

- All 3 and 5 Hp units using 208 or 220 Volt circuits are built to operate effectively from 187 volts to 253 volts.

- Split Phase = 1 phase with a start winding.

- No spark is allowed to occur in the rotor of a hermetic system. Therefore an outside control is used. Starting capacitors create a lead, which gives the motor a starting torque.

- Underwriters have checked klixons on hermetic motors under locked rotor conditions for a period of 15 days, 24 hours/day

- Klixon type protectors will open on a rise in temperature, caused either by actual heat of compressor or amperage within the line.

- Larger hermetics must have magnetic contactors in place of klixons.

- For each motor there is a starting capacitor, which will give a motor the greatest torque. All capacitors are rated in micro-farads.

- All capacitors are rated for so many 3 second starts per hour.

- 90 TW Hermetics have current type relays to remove starting capacitors from line

- 90 TG Hermetics have potential type relays to remove starting capacitors from line (surge open at 150 volt).

- All hermetics are built to run 10% above load on the nameplate.

- **Always** use time delay fuses for compressors, pumps and fan motors. Never one time fuses

- It is of vital importance to have the proper size fuses installed within the supply line in the event the compressor is in some way overloaded. The damage caused by a current overload is directly proportional to the size fuses or protectors in the line. A few seconds delay on tripout may mean the difference between a burn out motor or a repairable one.

- **Always** replace **all** fuses even if only one fuse fails. The others have been weakened and will cause problems in the future.

- An amprobe/voltmeter is, in reality, a transformer having a primary and a secondary coil. When placed within an electric field, a current is induced by electromagnetic induction.

- What substance has the greatest resistance to a current flow?

  ANSWER: Distilled water.

KEY NOTES AND GUIDELINES REGARDING COMPRESSORS

- **Compressors: (Open type)**

  - Prior to 1950, all compressors had aluminum covered lead gaskets (may be used again). When removing a motor, or for some reason disconnecting the terminal leads, always make sure the compressor shaft is turning in the same direction as before. This will prevent burrs on diaphragm and bearing surfaces from marring sealing surfaces which would, in turn, cause leaks within the seal.

  - NOTE: If the aluminum gaskets have been replaced, it is recommended that refrigeration oil be used on the gaskets for better sealing quality and ease of gasket removal if necessary.

- **Hermetics: (Sealed type - "can")**

  - Hermetic circuits (York) were brought out in 1952. It enabled the buyer to purchase refrigeration and air conditioning equipment more inexpensively.

  - No hermetic is repaired in the field. Put together by induction brazing at the factory.

  - Much trouble was encountered with leaks around the terminal lugs. This was caused by makers using the wrong type of rubber lugs. For this reason, when leaks are detected around these terminals, do not use a pressure greater than 7 lbs to tighten them.

- On new type hermetics, noise mufflers are on both suction and discharge lines in unit.

- In 1952 only .3% of hermetic compressors had mechanical failure.

- R-11 was used only on rotary or centrifugal type compressors (has almost the same R.E. as Carrene).

- 2 types of Hermetics: Air cooled and gas cooled

   - Low torque motor on fixture units.

   - High torque motor on low temperature units

- New Hermetics not made for 1/4 H.P. applications (in 1952)

- **Compressor H.P. ratings per ton**

- Evaporator Temperature = 40 F then H.P. per ton = 0.9

- Evaporator Temperature = 25 F then H.P. per ton = 1.1

- Evaporator Temperature = -5 F then H.P. per ton = 2.0

- Evaporator Temperature = -35 F then H.P. per ton = 3.0

- Evaporator Temperature = -65 F then H.P. per ton = 4.5

- Evaporator Temperature = -95 F then H.P. per ton = 6.0

   - **Example:** Room temp. = -125 F, 6 tons of refrigeration needed: 160 H.P.

KEY NOTES & GUIDELINES REGARDING REFRIGERATION & BRAZING

- Limit the height of the condenser above the evaporator if possible. **Reason:** Lower pressure drop and better oil circulation

- Never put unit in room with lower temperature than space to be refrigerated.

- When evacuating a unit, use pump rated for at least 150 microns (29.5")

- Do not use a compressor as a pump if good results are to be obtained. Make a system clean, make it tight and forget about it.

- Micron: = 1,000,000 of 1 meter.

- Wet bulb thermometer used to check vacuum prior to the micron type gauge.

- Use dry nitrogen to remove moisture after system is pumped down to 29.5".

- Also use dry nitrogen through lines when brazing. (prevents carbon formation)

  - Brazing guidelines - difference between brazing, soldering and welding

    - Lead solder melts between 400 F to 700 F

    - High Temperature braze melts between 1100 F to 1300 F (also Silfos)

    - Welding melts between 1800 F to 2500 F

- You can braze brass to copper. Better to braze without flux

- Discharge check valves were installed to prevent migration of refrigerant during the off cycle to the compressor heads and ultimately the evaporator. **Result:** Compressor protection from liquid slugging and compressor failure on start up.

- Recycling pump down to prevent excessive refrigerant build up in the low side evaporator and possible liquid slugging on compressor start up.

- Types of liquid controllers (refrigeration metering devises)

  - Hand expansion valves, used mainly on ammonia systems or as auxiliaries on same

  - Automatic expansion valve (constant pressure) primarily used on dairy equipment and ice cream equip. (Operates with two pressures - suction and spring. Suction works against spring pressure.)

- Thermal expansion valve

- High pressure float regulator

- Low pressure float regulator

- Capillary tube. Length of capillary determines velocity (pressure drop). Bore determines amount of refrigerant.

- **There are two types of thermal valves: Internal and externally equalized.**

  - **Internal:** An internally equalized thermal valve has three forces working within it. Bellows pressure, spring pressure and evaporator pressure. The evaporator pressure is the pressure of the gas as it enters the evaporator. It can be used when no pressure drop exists within the line.

  - **External**: An externally equalized thermal valve also has the same forces working upon it. However, the evaporator pressure, instead of being felt directly at the valve, or inlet side of the evaporator is picked up at the outlet side of the evaporator. This is done by means of a 1/4 " copper line extending from the thermal valve to the outlet side of the coil. This type valve is used when a pressure drop exists within the coil. Pressure drop within the evaporator is directly related with the superheat setting of the thermal valve. With a drop in pressure, there will be a corresponding drop in temperature. Since a thermal bulb reacts on temperature there would be a premature metering of the thermal valve, thereby cutting down the efficiency of the valve and the capacity of the evaporator. By using the external equalized thermal valve the true superheat could be obtained, thereby increasing the capacity of the evaporator.

- **Thermal expansion valve - most commonly used as a refrigeration metering device**

  - A thermal expansion valve is a metering device used to produce the maximum efficiency from an evaporator by governing the quantity of refrigerant passing through it. It also, to some extent, prevents refrigerant in liquid form from reaching the compressor and causing serious damage to internal parts. Although the automatic expansion valve has the same function and purpose in regards to evaporator performance and liquid slugging, its practicability is limited. An automatic expansion valve knows but one function and that is to maintain a constant pressure within the evaporator. This type valve is practically useless when it is called upon to control pressure within the evaporator. It will actually close when a heavy load is placed upon it. On the other hand, the thermal expansion valve will meter the refrigerant in accordance with the load within the box. This is obtained by means of a capillary tube on the top of the thermal expansion valve. The pressure exerted downward on the thermal valve is directly proportional to the temperature of the coil outlet. Two forces within the valve work against the downward pressure of the bellows. They are spring and evaporator pressure. If the refrigerant is allowed to flow through the coil in a liquid state, the pressure within the bellows and the evaporator pressure (barring pressure drop within the line or coil) would be the same. Therefore, the determining factor in regards to the superheat will be the spring tension against the bellows. The greater the spring tension, the higher the superheat.

  - The liquid charge in the thermal bulb is enough so that when the pressure reaches its maximum; there will still be a small quantity of liquid in the bulb no matter what the temperature around the thermal bulb. On a gas filled bulb the expansion valve must be in a warmer location than the bulb. (This is to prevent, in the event the temp. drops low enough to liquefy the gas, the liquid from settling on the bellows, causing erratic operation of the valve.)

- In reference to liquid filled thermal bulbs, there is no more positive action obtained when the capillary line is entirely filled with liquid. There would be no cushioning effect and reaction on valve seat would be faster.

- **Capillary tube: used as a refrigeration metering device in most fraction H.P. systems**

  - A tubular coil about 50" long, with a diameter of 1/16" to the end of which is a thermal or reactor bulb. This bulb is attached to the outlet line of the evaporator. The other end of the capillary tube is attached to the bellows of the thermal valve. This circuit is completely sealed. Its main function is to to produce a pressure equal to the temperature at the bulb. This pressure is felt at the bellows of the thermal valve. This circuit is charged with a liquid refrigerant in most cases. (The charge is usually the same as that within the system).

    - **Example:** For every refrigerant there is a definite temperature pressure relationship. At 0 lbs, the temperature of R-12 will be 21.7 F. This will only hold true when the refrigerant is in a liquid state. Only when the refrigerant is entirely gaseous will the temperature begin to rise. The temperature thus created is what acts upon the thermal bulb.

KEY NOTES AND GUIDELINES REGARDING OIL AND CRANK CASE HEATERS

- **Refrigeration oil**

  - Oil within a refrigeration system has but one function, and that is to lubricate the compressor.

  - Oil is pumped completely through the system and back to the compressor. Always check oil level after a compressor has been running for a while. This will allow you to get the true oil level in

---

the compressor. On larger systems a discharge oil separator is necessary. On these systems a surplus oil charge is not necessary. On prolonged shut downs, the refrigerant has a tendency of working its way to the compressor crankcase. On start up of the compressor, damage will occur. On large systems crankcase heaters are placed within the crankcase to prevent this.

- Oil comes in several viscosities and is used for different evaporator temperatures.

- **Crank case heaters**

  - When buying same, get a quality heater

  - Check surface temperature of heaters. (Should be between 120 F - 200 F).

  - Should have a 200 to 400 watt rating (on larger compressors).

  - When using compressors in multiple, always make oil equalizer lines the same size as the equalizer plugs in the compressor. **REASON:** To maintain oil levels in compressor crankcases.

  - If the velocity within a system is too low you will have a poor oil return to the compressor. This will also have an effect upon the amount of oil that will settle in the evaporator.

  - **NOTE:** The length, size and pitch of suction line plus compressor unloading can effect proper oil return to the compressor crankcase.

KEY NOTES AND GUIDELINES REGARDING AIR CONDITIONING, FANS AND AIR MOTION

- **Air-conditioning**

  - Defined as the change of the physical and chemical composition of air in an enclosure. It may also be defined as the simultaneous control of temperature, humidity, cleanliness, and air motion.

  - **It is divided into two phases: Summer and winter.**

John C. Schaub

- Summer: To decrease the temperature and humidity.

- Winter: To increase the temperature and humidity.

- Air is like a sponge. It can hold a certain amount of moisture. When it has absorbed all the moisture it can hold, it is said to be saturated.

- When the air contains less than the maximum amount of moisture it can hold, the quantity is expressed as a percentage of the maximum amount it can hold. This percentage is known as the relative humidity.

- The ability of air to absorb moisture depends upon its dry bulb temperature. The warmer the air becomes, the more moisture it can absorb before it reaches saturation, or 100% R.H.

- Dry bulb temperature: Temperature shown on an ordinary thermometer. (It is not a measure of the total heat of the air since it is not affected by the moisture content).

- Wet bulb temperature: Defined as the temperature of the air at saturation. When the air is saturated, the wet and dry bulb temperatures are the same.

- Absolute humidity: Defined as the absolute amount of water in the air. It is expressed in grains per pound, or grains per cubic foot. There are 7000 grains in 1 pound.

- Dew point temperature: Is the temperature at which moisture will begin to condense out of air which has a given amount of water vapor.

- **Fans:** There are three types of fans:

  - Propeller: If resistance be added, C.F.M. will be reduced, thereby reducing air to propeller. This will cause air to flow back through the center of fan, increasing wattage of motor.

  - Axial: Same design as propeller fan. However, the axial fan is so constructed as to prevent air from passing on a build up of air resistance, through center of fan. **REASON:** To prevent increase in wattage of fan motor as occurs in propeller fans.

- Centrifugal: A cylindrical, disk shaped fan, with blades running parallel to axis. On an increase in air resistance there is no increase in wattage.

- **Air motion and distribution:**

  - Defined as the movement of the correct quantity of air to the right places at the right time

  - Air distribution is the least studied part of the refrigeration system.

  - Sheet metal screws should not be on inside of duct cause noise and friction).

  - All elbows should have sufficient radius and size.

  - Any obstruction increases pressure in duct which works against air being pushed through.

  - All edges of metal should have tear drop design.

- **Rule of thumb guidelines and formulas for refrigeration tonnage:**

  - One ton of refrigeration = 400 C.F.M of air needed through the evaporator.

  - One ton of refrigeration = 800 C.F.M. of air through the condenser.

  - One ton of refrigeration = 3 G.P.M. water through water cooled condenser.

  - One ton of refrigeration = 2.4 G.P.M. (minimum) water through chilled water evaporator.

  - **Tons** = (T. D. x lbs. H20)/250 (water cooled condenser tons - chillers or AC systems).

    - T.D. is temperature difference of condenser water in and out.

    - Lb. H20 (water) = pounds of water flow per minute.

- 250 is BTU rating used for water cooled condensers
- NOTE: if G. P. M. flow is known, multiply 8.3 (Gallons of Water) x G. P. M.

- **Tons** = (T. D. x lbs. H20)/200 (water cooled evaporator tons-chillers only)

  - T.D. is temperature difference of evaporator water in and out.
  - 200 BTU's (water evaporator rating)
  - Lbs. H20 (water) = pounds of water flow per minute.
  - Pump curves could be used to determine water flow rate, however the accuracy changes the exact tons.
  - NOTE: if G.P.M. flow is known, multiply 8.3 (Gallons of Water) x G.P.M.

- **Formula review:**

  - B.T.U. = W x S.H. x T.D (Heat load = weight x specific heat x temperature difference)
  - B.T.U. = W x L.H. (Heat load = weight x latent heat)
  - R.E. = H.C.V. - H.C.L. (Refrigerating effect = Heat content of vapor - Heat content of liquid.)
  - Ton ref./min. = W. x S.H x (T1 - T2) / 200 (BTU's)
  - Condenser tons = G.P.M.'s x S.H. x (t1 - t2)
  - Evaporator tons = G.P.M.'s x S.H. x 9t1 - t2)/24
  - G. P.M.'s / water =30 x tons /range of water (t1 - t2)
  - Refrigerant circulated per minute = 200 x tons load / R.E.
  - C.F.M of refrigerant = Pi RxR x H. r.p.m. x No. cyl. x 75 / 1728 (# cubic. inches in a cubic foot)
  - Velocity in Ft./Min. =(Lb ref./min. x specific volume) /cross section suction line in sq. ft.

- Ratio of Compression =(Head pressure + 14.7) /(Back pressure + 14.7) Example: (250 + 14.7) / (65 + 14.7) = 3.32 R.C.

- Total Tons = C.F.M x (Th1 - Th2) / (13.8 x 200) --This is total heat.

- Sensible Tons = C.F.M x .24 x T.D./(13.8 x 200) --This is dry bulb.

- Latent Tons = C.F.M x (.Ah1 - .Ah2) x 1060/ (13.8 x 7000 x 200) A.H = absolute humidity

- Latent Heat / lb = (A.H x 1060)/ 7000 A.H. = grains of moisture removed.

Chapter 5

TROUBLE SHOOTING

Phyllis Diller, the comedian, was quoted as saying, "Marriage is great. However, no one told me about the garbage and the laundry."

All professions have latent difficulties as most HVAC/R technicians can attest. Only upon visiting hundreds of "sick" systems on emergency calls will you shorten your correction time relative to the problem.

Educational schools, societies, and manufacturers have contributed volumes of knowledge in this field. Few, however can be reached at 2:00AM. In the past decade, innovations used to find the problem have quickened the repair time. About 80% of the existing systems are still chugging away without this luxury. Meanwhile, until systems can talk, you are the person to resolve the problem.

This chapter will touch on the following "how to" list of service troubleshooting and repairs. The sections I have included are the basics of how to address these problems.

1. Emergency Service Situations

2. Preventative Maintenance Lists

3. Low Refrigerant Pressure (Air and Water Cooled)

4. High Refrigerant Pressure (Air Cooled)

5. High Refrigerant Pressure (Water Cooled)

6. Oil Failure

7. Freezestat and Flow Switch

8. Refrigerant Leak Repair

---

9. Technical Info

10. Public Relations and Pricing

11. Electrical

12. Superheat and Subcooling

13. Compressor Change-outs

14. Heat Pumps

15. Heating

16. Start up procedures for new chiller system

17. Tower System Start Up Procedures

18. Checks before condemning any compressor or motor.

---

1. EMERGENCY SERVICE CALLS

A. The first step is to speak to those most familiar with the system operation. It is surprising the information that can be obtained from the office or plant workers who are directly responsible for operating the production machines. Workers who come in early or leave late can also see things that can help you make the correct assessment. Remember, they are present on a daily basis and can hear or see things vital to your search for the problem.

B. Compressor Room – It is advised a plant maintenance worker accompany you here for guidance and any input he can offer relative to system history. Again, time will be saved on this project. Depending on your findings, many initial tests can be eliminated. However, if you find the compressor off and the main control on, shut off the main power switch and control power source until all fuses have been checked. In the event of a blown compressor fuse, the compressor (or motor) leads must be disconnected at the terminal and the windings are checked for grounds.

NOTE: All time lag fuses used on motors are limited to about eight starts per hour depending on the room temperature and the size of the fuse. Compressor "short cycling" sometimes causes this event.

C. Safety Controls – 80% of emergency service calls are caused by manual reset safety controls. They bring attention to a more serious problem which must be addressed immediately to save more costly repairs. As a certified technician, you can handle the reasons and the cure.

D. Solving emergency calls via phone – Given the correct data by the technician at the job site, correction of the problem can often be done. However, it is advised NOT to guide someone over the phone to do troubleshooting for you if he or she does not know what they are doing.

E. Diplomacy – The longer it takes to arrive at the job site, the angrier the customer will be. At this moment try to be understanding!

---

2. PREVENTATIVE MAINTENANCE INSPECTION LISTS

Depending on the type of refrigeration equipment, different preventative maintenance services are performed. Following is a general list of what to do for all refrigeration systems and some specifics for systems like chillers and air conditioning systems.

Preventative Maintenance Services (Basic Inspections)

- Take Model and Serial Number of unit.

- Talk with the person most closely involved with starting or checking the system.

- Install gauges to compressor(s) and oil pressure, (if able to do so).

- Attach temperature probes to measure superheat and subcooling.

- Write down thermostat setting before you begin your inspections.

- Check and write down the major safety settings.

- Check electrical connections, contactors and electrical components for proper tightness and wiring.

- Measure amperages and voltages. (Make sure they correspond to proper ratings.)

- Check suction and discharge pressures.

- Check refrigerant and oil charges.

- If air cooled, check all condensers coils and air filters.

- Visually inspect lines for rubbing and vibration.

- Visually inspect for refrigerant and oil leaks.

- Verify that thermostat settings are accurate when the system starts and shuts off.

- Provide and explain the detailed report of the work you have performed.

PREVENTATIVE MAINTENANCE SERVICES – CHILLER INSPECTIONS

- Take Model and Serial Number of unit.

- Talk with the person(s) most closely involved with starting or checking the system.

- Install gauges to compressor(s) and oil pressure (if able to do so)

- Attach temperature probes to measure superheat and subcooling.

- Write down thermostat setting before you begin your inspections.

- Inspect to see if this chiller is air cooled or water cooled.

- Inspect the tower system (if water cooled) which is also part of the maintenance of a chiller.

- Towers will have an outdoor evaporative or ambient cooling section which may include a fan, filters and screen.

- Tower systems also have an indoor tank that will have water treatment (hopefully) along with pumps screens and filters. Inspect all of these items. The water treatment is usually done by a professional who knows water treatment.

- Check tower water pressure entering the nozzles or main header, along with the water sprays to be sure no clogging has occurred.

- Check and write down the major safety settings and tower water settings.

- Additional safeties such as water flow switch, pump amperage overloads, freezestat and low water level must also be inspected on a chiller system.

- Check electrical connections, contactors and electrical components throughout the system.

- Measure amperages and voltages. (Make sure they correspond to proper ratings.)

- Check refrigeration suction and discharge pressures.

- Check refrigerant and oil charges.

- Measure antifreeze (if used). Make sure that the antifreeze used covers the possible freezing of the coldest temperature that the water/antifreeze mixing will touch. That could be the evaporator or could be the outdoor weather temperatures – if the chiller is located outside. Remember to make sure the safety margin is about 10F less than the coldest temperature.

- Check all condenser coils, if air cooled, and check air filters.

- Visually inspect lines for rubbing and vibration.

- Visually inspect for refrigerant and oil leaks.

- Verify that thermostat settings are accurate when the system starts and shuts off.

- Provide and explain the detailed report of the work you have performed

PREVENTATIVE MAINTENANCE SERVICES (AIR-CONDITIONING)

- Take Model and Serial Number of unit.

- Talk with person in the area that is air-conditioned and ask how things "feel".

- Install gauges to compressor.

- Attach temperature probes to measure superheat and subcooling.

- Write down thermostat setting before you begin your inspections.

- Check electrical connections contactors and electrical components.

- Measure amperages and voltages. (Make sure they correspond to proper ratings.)

- Check suction and discharge pressures.

- Check refrigerant charges. Remember that most AC units are not thermal valve, but are cap tube metering. The charge will depend on the discharge pressure

- Visually inspect lines for rubbing and vibration.

- Visually inspect for refrigerant and oil leaks.

- Verify that thermostat settings are accurate when the system starts and shuts off.

---

3. LOW REFRIGERANT PRESSURE (AIR AND WATER COOLED)

A. Shortage of refrigerant (find leak and repair).

B. Thermostat set too low (causing evaporator to ice up). Regarding a chiller (unit has antifreeze), check freeze point.

C. Evaporator iced or partially iced up - check for low suction and low superheat

   - De-ice evaporator by turning compressor switch off, but leave

---

indoor blower fan "on" or for a chiller leave the process or recirculation pump on.

- Find cause only after you have de-iced evaporator.

D. Evaporator coils dirty or clogged: for refrigeration systems, this is a visual check. For chillers, check Delta T under full load to see if you have at least 10°F spread (low suction, low superheat) in and out of evaporator (water).

E. Ruptured power element

- To check for this, take power element bulb and hold it in your hand. If no change in suction pressure, power element is defective.

- Look for frost and ice on external equalizer line. This means that liquid refrigerant is traveling through equalizer line. Power element either has lost some of its charge or is starting to become defective.

- Low suction or no suction (high superheat).

F. Liquid Line Solenoid Valve -- Coil burned out, valve stuck closed or sticking.
Note: Take valve apart and check for ridge or rim caused by wear.

G. Chillers only - Incorrect sizing of water lines causes a reduced GPM flow as per manufacturer's specs; 2.4 to 3 GPM per ton. On most chillers there should be a water bypass line that should be cracked 10 to 15%.

H. Water regulating valve below 90°F condensing temperature when full loaded causing low suction pressure. Note: Low discharge – low suction.

I. Process Pump – Rotation of pump incorrect, shorted, fuses blown, overload tripped.

J. Check to see if liquid line shut off valve is closed.

- Check to see if Y-strainer is clogged which would result in reduced GPM through evaporator.

- Slime build up in evaporator – use water valving procedures to clear it or acid flush.

K. Clogged dryer (feel inlet and outlet of dryer) – If there is a temperature difference the dryer is clogged, restricting refrigerant flow, causing low suction pressure. You will feel a cool liquid line. High superheat (25-30°F) - no matter how you adjust the thermal valve. Might not feel a temperature difference across the dryer in this case.

L. Chillers only - Make sure all water line valves are open (check for Y-strainer screens).

M. Chillers only - Crushed tubes in evaporator - should have a approximately 10 pound pressure drop from inlet to outlet water line of evaporator) Note: Should have at least 10°F superheat.

N. Inoperative LP control (out of calibration, capillary hooked up on high side or oil pump pressure).

O. No refrigerant in system (unit will not run).

P. Improperly set superheat - evaporator too cold and icing occurs.

Q. Room temperature not 70°F+ (air cooled only)

This causes low discharge pressure causing low suction pressure. If unit has fan cycling, check for proper adjustment or setting. If unit does not have fan cycling control, recommend to customer to have one installed. (This problem happens in the cooler months.)

R. Low pressure safety trips due to low outside temperatures

(Note: Refrigerant will be the same temperature as the outside ambient air temperature.)

- Lower low pressure safety's cut in and cut out lower than outside ambient air temperature.

- Check to see if low pressure safety has a time delay. If so, you may need to increase the time so the suction pressure increases to proper pressures.

S. Unit will go off on low pressure if wired to go off by a pump down sequence. Unit may not come on if low pressure cut in setting is set too high or set lower than L.P. safety.

---

4. HIGH REFRIGERANT PRESSURES (AIR COOLED)

A. Dirty condenser filters or coils - clear or wash.

B. Evaporators process air too hot - cool room down by ventilation first if possible. If this is not possible, valve back the air flow until the unit can handle the heat load.

Chillers – water too hot – rectify by valving back on outlet water from evaporator. If no valve outlet, valve back on return water.

C. Unit placed in room that is too hot.

D. Loose belt on blower wheel or fan motor.

E. Condenser fan motor not working – Contactor heater tripped, shorted, fuses blown

F. Unit overloaded (load more than unit is designed to handle).

G. Fan cycling control defective or capillary line hooked up on low side. This is rare but possible.

H. Defective HP safety (out of calibration or hooked up on low side).

I. Unit overcharged (see subcooling)

J. Discharged air being recirculated back through condenser coil.

K. Condenser fan motor running backwards.

L. Insufficient air flow through condenser coil

   • Check for proper ventilation in and out of room. Place rag on condenser coil to see if there is proper air flow.

- Check damper positioning to see if discharged air is dead heading itself.

M. Blower wheel blade cups filled with dirt, reducing air flow.

N. Duct work should only be done for blower wheels, not prop fans, because they are not designed to take the back pressure the duct work creates.

5. HIGH REFRIGERANT PRESSURE (WATER COOLED)

A. Dirty condenser

- Check inlet and outlet water lines – should have a temperature difference.

- Condenser's gasket could have been put on incorrectly on shell and tube ends.

B. Unit is over charged (check subcooling).

C. Unit over loaded (load more than unit is designed to handle)

D. Defective HP (high pressure) safety

- Safety out of calibration

- Check to see if capillary is hooked on the high side

E. Problem with cooling tower

- Belt broken or loose on tower fan motor

- Tower dirty causing improper water flow

    1) Check spray nozzles to see if they are clear

    2) Check to see if return water line is blocked with debris or dirt at reservoir at the bottom of the tower.

- T-stat for tower defective or setting improperly adjusted.

- Check tower's filter media to see if it is clean (feel top of tower inlet water and outlet water to see if there is a good Delta T)

John C. Schaub

- Check to see if tower pump is on, and check for blown fuses.

- Check for proper rotation of fan or blower wheel

F. Water regulating valve (most units have these) mainly on chiller systems.

- Not adjusted properly; valve stuck; slow leak in capillary or broken capillary line causing valve to stay shut.

G. Insufficient water flow through condenser

- Tower pump shorted

- Inlet of tower pump clogged with debris

- Check for proper rotation of pump

- Check for blown fuses

- Pump's contactors overload tripped

- Check out water regulating valve

- Tower pump not large enough

- Water lines not sized properly going to and from condenser

- Check water line for Y-strainer – could be dirty causing reduced water flow

H. Chiller only - Chilled water entering evaporator too hot - too much heat load that condenser cannot remove. Valve back on the evaporator water and keep an eye on the suction gauge. Make sure the suction gauge does not go to the "icing" state while the water is slowly lowered in temperature. This should keep the high side pressure low enough not to trip.

I. Unit trips off on HP safety only on initial start up.

- Initial water regulating opening swing trips the high head pressure by letting in too much warm water.

- Hot water from overhead tower lines due to tower being far away (because water flow is not continuous). Tower water bypass needed at condensers inlet and outlet water lines, to insure proper inlet temperature on start up.

J. Air in system - very rare but possible if not properly evacuated. With compressor off (through condenser only)

- Refer to pressure temperature chart for R-22 or other refrigerants

  a) water temperature should match refrigerant temperature (water cooled)

  b) air temperature should match refrigerant temperature (air cooled)

K. Original or replacement sizing problems: Either oversized evaporator or undersized condenser coil.

---

6. OIL FAILURE

A. Insufficient oil (check compressor sight glass)

B. Liquid refrigerant entering the compressor washing away oil.

- Unit iced up

- Superheat too close

C. Oil pump seized or beginning to seize. Check oil pressure to be at least 20 psig above suction pressure. The exact oil pressure difference will depend on the compressor.

D. Oil safety trips on initial start ups only

- Crankcase heater shut off overnight or not working.

- Liquid refrigerant weeping into the compressor through hot gas, broken valves, liquid line solenoid valve; or room temperature too cold.

E. Defective oil failure safety or capillaries hooked up improperly.

F. Clogged oil strainer (large compressors only) Screen for oil pump located in crankcase of compressor.

G. Broken down oil (low viscosity, oil black) change oil and check for acid in system

H. Oil logged evaporator due to prolonged unloaded conditions and poor piping design. Full load for 30 minutes and see if all the oil returns to the crank case.

I. Running too cold without proper antifreeze protection.

J. Not enough flow (minimum 2.4 GPM per ton) causing low super-heat

7. FREEZESTAT & FLOW SWITCH - CHILLER WATER SYSTEM ONLY

FREEZESTAT

A. Thermostat set too low or freezestat set too high. Freezestat should be set 10 to 15°F lower than thermostat.

B. Unit iced up (bulb may be located where ice is, not necessarily the true water temperature).

C. Freezestat out of calibration or defective.

D. Check water flow (minimum 2.4 GPM per ton).

E. Power element bulb should be well insulated.

F. Freezestat bulb is always located on outlet of evaporator – never on return water line.

G. Check to make sure bulb straps are tight.

H. A freezestat should always be a manual reset on a chiller - never automatic.

FLOW SWITCH

A. Flow switch with broken paddles, turbulent water flow, water valve at the outlet of the evaporator, not choked back properly.

B. No water flow (iced evaporator, valves at machines shut off, clogged evaporator inlet, pump rotation incorrect or not running at all).

C. Flow switch should always be on the outlet of the evaporator.

D. Arrow on flow switch should always be in the direction of the water flow.

E. Check pump contactor – overload could be tripped due to over amperage.

8. REFRIGERATION LEAK REPAIR-STEP BY STEP

A. Locate leak using Halide, Bubble or Electronic leak detectors. Be sure to bubble the leak to pinpoint its location. If necessary, scratch the copper line to indicate exact location so that it can be found after the area has been cleaned up.

B. If leak is a flare, thread or compressor fitting, tighten and recheck. This enables you to not have to recover any refrigerant or pump down the system.

C. Determine whether the leak is on the high side or low side refrigerant lines.

E. If leak is on the low side, shut off liquid line service valve (king valve) and proceed to pump down unit by activating compressor contactor. Remember if this system is a screw or a scroll this cannot be done due to the fact that refrigerant will pass by from the high side to the low side and refill the low side with refrigerant. Complete recovery is necessary in these instances.

- Low pressure safety may need to be lowered if the compressor contactor cannot be manually held in. Bring low pressure side down to 4 psig or less (multiple compressor starts may be necessary). When pressure is staying constant (less than 5 psig), open suction port and properly remove any remaining refrigerant. Leaving the suction side open, repair the leak. Without opening the king valve, use refrigerant to pressurize the low side and check for any

THE LIFE OF AN HVAC/R TECHNICIAN

leaks. If no leaks are found, proceed to evacuate low side. After evacuation, open all valves, restart unit and check for leaks one more time.

F. High pressure leaks

- No pumping down can be done to isolate refrigerant when leak is on the high side. Hook up recovery equipment and remove all refrigerant from high side and low side.

- Repair leak, pressurize, leak test and evacuate system (both sides). Recharge system with recovered refrigerant. Restart unit and leak test one more time.

G. Leaks found on the compressor (high or low sides)

- Shut off power to compressor. Valve off both suction and discharge service valves and properly remove the refrigerant in the compressor. Repair leak and follow above procedures as to the start up and check out.

---

9. TECHNICAL INFORMATION - RULE OF THUMB (CHILLERS AND HVAC SYSTEMS)

A. Water Flow Sizing

- Water cooled condensers: 3 gallons per ton per minute

- Water cooled evaporators: 2.4 (minimum) gallons per ton per minute

- One gallon of water = 8.3 lb; 10 gallons = 83 lb.

B. Tonnage Ratings

- Chillers: Tonnage ratings are generally calculated at 45°F supply water temperature.

- For every 1 degree drop in temperature, there is a 2% loss of overall tonnage.

- Example: supply water 45°F with a 10 ton unit 55 − 45 = 10° = an

John C. Schaub 79

8 ton unit 10 x 2% = 20% less tonnage. Unit is now an eight ton unit. The same is true for every degree rise in temperature up to about 10% increased tonnage.

- Tonnage calculation formula (10° x 2% = 2 tons loss of tonnage)

C. Injection Molding Heat Sizing:

- Ask type of plastic used and how much material per hour used Rule of Thumb ratings:

Polypropylene (85% of all plastics)	30 lb. materials per ton
Nylon	40 lb. materials per ton
PVC	65 lb. materials per ton

- Ask horsepower of motor used if chiller is being used for cooling hydraulic oil.

  Rule of Thumb:

  10 horsepower = 1 ton of refrigeration or 50 horsepower = 5 tons, etc.

D. To calculate tonnage of a chiller- obtain these items and then refer to "equations"

- Obtain Delta T of the evaporator water or condenser water.

- Measure water flow exiting the evaporator in GPM (gallons per minute).

E. Equation: Superheats – A/C Units   12° to 15°F

    Chillers 10° to 12°F

- NOTE: superheat is very relative and depends on the evaporator temperature range. Standard home or commercial air conditioning systems have a 10 to 20F superheat. Refrigeration systems can have anywhere from 10F all the way down to 2F (low temp -30F freezers). Chillers have the same reasoning; it all depends on how cold the evaporator is going to get. The colder the evaporator the closer the superheat will become.

John C. Schaub

F. Ductwork – Do not run ductwork for propeller fans for chillers. They are not designed to take the back pressure.

G. Electrical amperages – running amps of any motor if not posted are approximately $1/6^{th}$ of the LRA (locked rotor amps) rating (Example: LRA=74 Running amps (RLA) = 74 ÷ 6 = 12.1 amps

H. Compressor temperatures:

- Discharge gas physical line temperature between 160-180 F.

- Try to keep the discharge temperatures below 200F

- Oil breakdown temperature begins where either the discharge line gas temperature is around 240F or lower if the oil has any moisture to lower its breakdown capability. Actual piston temperatures are 75- 100F hotter than the discharge line gas temperature measured off the compressor. Actual oil breakdown, with good oil, occurs around 325F.

I. Oil pressures: Although each compressor manufacturer tells what the necessary oil pressure (above suction pressure) is required, most need at least 20 psi above to keep the compressor well lubricated.

J. Oil level: Again another area that will depend not only on the compressor manufacturer, but the compressor body itself. Some bodies are designed to hold a great deal in the crank case. Others do not have a crank case (some screws) and others have a small level area for the oil- Example: Copeland 8D model style, which requests only a ¼ full glass when running.

- NOTE: If the oil gets too high in the level, the pistons rocker arms can hit the oil and cause high amps in the compressor.

K. Voltages: All units have a range of operating voltages. some from 40 years ago are rated at 440 volts while the newer one of today are at 480 volts. It does not matter what voltage you run; but it is important that the voltages are correct with in a standard and balanced within standard

- No less or no more than 10% of the rated voltage

- No more than 2% unbalance between phases

---

10. PRICING AND PUBLIC RELATIONS

PRICING

A. Fair trade mark up is what a contractor charges the customer above the cost of the part. In most cases the mark up can range anywhere from 10% to 100% depending on what is being sold. Large central systems come closer to the 10% mark up where by select OEM components can get upwards of 100%.

B. OEM pricing and account privileges are something that the manufacturers will dictate to only a few specialized companies. Be aware that the contractor is at the mercy of their price gradients and the prices from these manufacturers may be higher than normal. Although it is just and the part will be an identical replacement in most cases; be aware that the price will be higher.

C. Shipping prices have been a sector that is also up to the shipping companies and the rising oil prices for gasoline have not helped the rising costs. Many customers need to have that "special" part yesterday and are willing to pay for that to happen. When it comes to chillers and the production sector, having a part "next day air" is the norm since they losing sometimes thousands of dollars per day due to the downtime. Now with air conditioning, you may have someone that says just to send it "regular ground." The best piece of advice is to tell the customer what the options are up front and let them know that the pricing for the shipping is an "estimate" only.

D. Refrigerant prices have been long changing and the EPA has created the most recent change in the last decade. Prices of refrigerant will fluctuate from month to month. New refrigerants are being created and tested. Be ready to check your local distributors' prices from month to

---

month to make sure that your pricing is the industry standard for most out there.

CUSTOMER PUBLIC RELATIONS

A. Always get name (first then last with correct spelling) of your contact.

B. If new account, get address, phone number, E-mail and directions (ask if PO# is required)

C. We guarantee all work for 30 days except discharge brazing repairs. If unit manufacturer gives more than 1 year with the warranty items, then pass that on to the customer.

D. New installations of compressors, parts of new units – parts under warranty one year.

E. Present yourself as confident and clean. Listen, it will be your best tool.

F. Include personnel in all the work you do and teach them whenever they wish.

G. Be patient, patient, patient and present findings (problems, etc) only when you are ABSOLUTELY SURE of what you have found!

11. ELECTRICAL - TROUBLESHOOTING TECHNIQUES

A. **High Voltage 460/230 volts – single & three phase**

1. Checking for grounds and shorts

    •   When checking any motor or electrical device, shut off main power and verify with volt meter. Remove all leads at closest point to the motor. Using continuity tester, check each wire or lead to the ground. If there is continuity, motor is shorted. Even only one shorted wire means motor is shorted.

    •   Do not check wires of contactor because there could be a break in the wire between contactor and motor causing a false reading.

2. Checking for Continuity

    • Same as above for shutting off and checking for power, along with removing wires closest to motor. With am-probe on continuity, check across each wire (from wire to wire at the same time). Check all combinations from wire to wire. Every combination should have continuity. If any combination does not have continuity it is considered to have an open winding, and must be replaced.

    • Some motors have internal overloads that open automatically due to extreme heat. A true continuity test should be redone when the motor is cool.

3. How to check fuses - these practices pertain to any fuse of any voltage.

    • With power off, pull fuse and check from one end to the other with the continuity tester (No continuity – blown fuse).

    • With power on, check the entering side with the volt meter to ground and check the other side of the fuse to see if it has voltage also. (No voltage; blown fuse)

4. How to check and replace a capacitor

    • Visually puffed or swollen, leaking fluid, change immediately.

    • Using voltmeter put one lead on one side of capacitor and other lead on other side of capacitor. Check for proper microfarad reading (depends on size of capacitor).

    • An old trade trick is also (carefully) remove capacitor without touching the two prongs at the same time. With an analog voltmeter on "voltage setting", touch each prong with the voltmeter leads. A small "spike" should register on your voltmeter. If you touch across the capacitor with a metal object before you do this test, it will not show up.

- Short across the two prongs with an insulated tool. This will remove the charge that would have given you a "shock". Then remove and replace the capacitor exactly as it was wired.

5. Check for even voltage supply in unit.

- Make sure all connections are tight.

- With volt meter, check each leg to leg. There should be no more than 2% deviation from the voltage coming into each leg.

B. Low Voltage 120 and 24 volt AC

1. Most control voltage starts from the step down transformer and follows a series path through switches and safeties to eventually energize the coil of a contactor, starter or relay. Low voltage also controls solenoid valves and panel lights.

2. A low voltage open circuit can be caused by:

- A direct short causing the control fuse to blow.

- An open safety due to other problems.

- Loose connections.

3. How to follow control voltage:

- Using volt meter, starting from transformer (power side), follow voltage from wire to wire until open is found. Low voltage application in module boards, circuit boards, etc. must be checked with a DC volt meter only (rarely necessary in our applications).

- If unit has blown fuses, check contactor to see if contacts have been fused together. If you cannot check visually, then use amprobe to check for a fused contact.

- Example: High voltage measuring

1-2	475
1-3	480
2-3	<u>485</u>

    $1440 \div 3 = 480$
    .02 x 480 = 9.6 volts deviation allowed
    max deviation from this average only 5v.

---

12. SUPERHEAT AND SUBCOOLING

A. Superheat:

- The temperature difference between the refrigerant entering and leaving the evaporator at the same pressure. The temperature entering the evaporator is found on the suction gauge pressure temperature line of whatever the refrigerant is in the system.

- The temperature exiting the evaporator is measured by a temperature probe, either strapped or infrared, at the closest point exiting the evaporator.

- Normal superheat readings are taken under full load and design temperatures:

a) Chillers:	10 to 12°F
b) Air conditioners:	14 to 16°F
c) Air Driers:	per manufacturers design

- The lower the water or air temperatures the lower the superheat. If a chiller or refrigeration unit runs at 5F, the superheat may only be 5F.

- If superheat is too close (depending on the conditional temperatures) possibly too much refrigerant is being fed into the evaporator.

- If superheat is too far apart (depending on the conditional temperatures), possibly not enough refrigerant is being fed into evaporator.

B. Subcooling:

- The temperature difference between the refrigerant's condensing temperature (found on the discharge gauge pressure temperature line of whatever refrigerant used) and the temperature exiting the condenser (liquid line); both of which have the same pressure.

- Subcooling is measured by – Taking the condensing temperature that is found on the discharge gauge pressure line of whatever refrigerant used and subtracting it from the exiting temperature that is measured with a temperature probe strapped to the liquid line exiting the condenser.

- Normal subcooling temperatures are (10-20°F). This is uniform no matter what conditional temperatures. If subcooling is less, (0 to 10°F), unit is possibly short of refrigerant. If subcooling is greater than 30°F, unit is possibly overcharged.

---

13. COMPRESSOR CHANGE-OUTS - STEP BY STEP PROCEDURES.

A. Initial questions to ask.

- What kind of compressor is it?

- Do we have compressor service valves to isolate the refrigerant in the compressor from the rest of the refrigerant in the system?

- What type of compressor - semi-hermetic, hermetic, scroll or screw?

- What kind of refrigerant is in the system?

- Is the new compressor an identical replacement or do you have to retro fit the lines?

- What is our main voltage coming into the unit?

- Do you know if it is a "break up" or "burnout"

B. Burn out semi-hermetic (steps)

1. Shut off main power and lock it out

2. Trip high pressure safety and turn T-stat all the way up.

3. Valve off service valves to isolate refrigerant between compressor and system (after gauges are installed)

4. Recover contaminated refrigerant from compressor only. (Make sure to use drier with recovery unit.)

5. Disconnect and tag all wires. Make sure connect wires are not hot from an adjacent circuit (also crankcase heater wires).

6. Unbolt and pull away compressor service valves.

7. Remove and tag all capillary lines.

8. Remove crankcase heater only if it is a strap on (if possible).

9. Loosen all hold-down bolts for compressor.

10. Obtain in-house riggers if necessary to remove compressor.

11. Remove compressor hold-down bolts when rigging straps are in place.

12. Remove old and install new compressor in place. (Loosely install hold-down bolts.)

13. Reattach all capillaries and service valves.

14. Pressure test and evacuate compressor.

15. Tighten all hold-down bolts.

16. Attach superheat probe and oil pressure gauges.

17. Change out fuses and/or contactor if necessary. (Change all fuses if one was originally blown.)

18. Turn on main power and check voltages.

19. Set up voltmeter to measure amperage, reset HP safety. Lower the thermostat, if necessary, until compressor comes on.

20. Check all amperages, pressures, and refrigerant and oil charges. Add where necessary.

21. Take oil sample (if possible). If visually dirty, change oil until clear. Then take acid test. (Wait ½ hour between oil changes.)

22. Let run for 1 hour and change liquid line drier.

23. Make sure old and new model and serial numbers are obtained and that old compressor has been sealed and is ready for return.

24. Make final checks of superheat, oil, refrigeration charge, amperages and pressures at your set point temperature. Record all of the above mentioned items.

C. **Burnout "Can" or scroll compressor**

- Steps to be taken in order: 1, 2, 3… if compressor has no service valves, entire contaminated charge must be reclaimed.

- Steps 5 through 24 (in previous section)

- Rigger not necessary if compressor is small.

- Step 22 for "burn out" Let unit run for one hour and change liquid line drier. If unit has a bad burn, liquid line drier may have to be replaced again if it clogs within the next hour. It is also recommended to check again in a few days.

---

14. HEAT PUMPS - TROUBLESHOOTING

A. Winter in heating mode

- Dirty filters

- Evaporator fan motor not working (blower relay shorted)

- Reversing valve not shifting (could be shifter or coil – also in cooling season)

- Refrigerant shortage or overcharged

- Thermostat not working correctly

- Unit iced up (defrost control not working properly causing improper air flow)

- Blown fuses

- Return air blocked

- Delay timer not operating

- Defrost hose broken or clogged with ice

- Defrost switch not working

- Defrost sensor inoperative

- Module board defective

- Broken valves in compressor (low discharge and high suction)

- Condenser fan not working

- Debris under evaporator under outside coil causing improper air flow

- Inside diffusers closed

- Defective liquid line sensor (senses coil temperature)

- Snow and ice on top of outside condensing unit blocking air flow

- Defrost timer defective

- Clogged suction line filter

- Clogged liquid line drier

- Compressor off on internal overload

- Shortage of refrigerant (all units)
- Back up electric heat not energizing
  - T-stat problem
  - Electric heat contactor or relay
  - Broken electric heat coil

---

15. HEATING PROBLEMS - GAS FIRED

A. What to Look for:

- Clogged or dirty filters
- Loose belt or shorted fan motor
- Pilot out
- Defective thermocouple
- Spark igniter rusty at contacts
- Defective igniter
- End switch not working (sail switch)
- Draft motor not working
- Main gas valve not opening (shorted coil, diaphragm stuck, high limit switch open). Older units: pilot flame not strong enough to heat the thermocouple to start unit. Improper flame position.
- Blower fan time delay relay not working
- By-passed air getting into heat exchanger (yellow flame that is not able to be corrected)
- Thermostat not turned on to heating
- Flame rod broken or bent
- Outside air dampers open too much
- Control relay or heat relay not working

- Reset relay not working

- Older units mainly: flue pipe clogged with rust and particles.

- Gas not turned on

- Pilot orifice dirty

- Glow coil burned out (older units)

- Gas valve switch off (needs to be turned on)

- Pressure regulator vent tube clogged. If pilot flame does not light, check to see if gas pressure regulator has a vent tube copper line. Remove it and clean regulator and vent line. If vent line is dirty, the regulator will not sense atmospheric pressure at 14.7 psi and will not provide enough gas pressure for pilot tube to light. Also check pilot tube to see if it is clear after the vent tube is clean.

---

16. START UP PROCEDURE FOR NEW CHILLER SYSTEM

A. Write down M/N and S/N of unit.

B. Check name plate voltage and verify system as the right voltage connected to it.

C. Ask person in charge at plant if main power has been on for at least 24 hours for cc heater (crankcase heater) operation.

D. Check type of refrigerant used in system.

E. Check all shut off valves.

    a. Service valves for water regulating valves.

    b. Discharge service valve on compressor (this is VERY important).

    c. Suction service valve on compressor.

    d. Liquid line shut off valves.

F. Lock out compressors by tripping out a manual reset safety.

G. Check oil sight glass on semi-hermetic compressors to see if there is an oil level. If you cannot see it, or if you think oil level is above the glass, there could be liquid refrigerant in compressor. Ask person in charge how long cc heaters have been energized. It is not even worth trying to bump compressors or compressor. Come back the next day and check oil level in glass. By then all of the liquid refrigerant (or most of it) has been boiled off and then it should be okay to start. Also, some of the hermetic (can compressors) have an oil glass. This is more common on large can compressors.

H. **All pumps working with chiller** – before starting any pump, make sure the discharge shut off valve (mainly located above pump) is shut off 100% before turning it on. Once rotation is confirmed, start pumps and open valves *very* slowly (very important). Start up tower system if chiller is water cooled. (See tower start up procedures.) Check rotation of condenser fans if system is air cooled.

I. **Very important – applies if compressors are scroll or screw type.** When starting up scroll compressors that are three phase, they must run with the proper rotation. When you start up chiller system with these compressors, if they are NOT running in proper rotation there will be no pressure differential between the high side gauge and the low side gauge and they will be very noisy. Reverse the rotation by switching phases at each compressor contactor or preferably at main 3 phase terminal block coming into unit. After doing so, check rotation on chiller water pumps again and make phase changes if necessary at their contactors.

With screw compressors, phase checking is a must. The compressor will be immediately damaged if it runs in the reverse direction even for 1-2 seconds. Most chillers have a phase monitor built into the system. If it does not, please use the proper phase monitor to check before you start a screw compressor.

J. Check refrigeration safeties to see if they are set properly.

K. Install refrigeration gauges to system and superheat probes.

L. Once all checks stated above have been confirmed, you are ready to start up system. Always bump compressors first to make sure there is no liquid refrigerant in them. Note: This only applies to reciprocating compressors, not screws or scrolls.

M. Attach voltmeter - set for amperage measurement - on the compressor high voltage leads.

N. You may have to valve back on process and circulation water pumps for proper running amperages.

O. Very important checks to be done when system is running (especially with the full production load the system was designed to cool down).

    a.   Refrigerant pressures

    b.   Superheat, subcooling, discharge line temperature

    c.   Compressor amperages

    d.   Water flow rates

    e.   Oil pressure (on semi-hermetic or oil pump driven compressors)

    f.   Is Thermostat supply water or return water sensing

P. *Important:* If compressor is a large can style, look for an oil pressure Schrader fitting. If so, follow the manufacturer procedures on the sticker as to how to drain excess oil.

Q. Most of these start up procedures apply on small chiller systems also.

R. When you are finished, always call equipment manufacturer and inform them as to how start up proceeded.

S. Communicate to customer any recommendations you have on how system may run without any problems. For example, one of the most important things of all – **thermostat set point** (to prevent evaporator from ice ups). Alert them as to any other concerns or advice you may have (i.e., antifreeze freeze point of process water).

17. TOWER SYSTEM START UP PROCEDURES - FOR ALL WATER COOLED REFRIGERATION SYSTEMS

A. Write down M/N and S/N of tower system.

B. Check name plate voltage and verify system has the correct voltage coming to it.

C. Check all water piping and how it is run as well as piping sizes.

D. **Important:** Make sure on tower reservoir tank that circulation water line going up to tower has a bleed off water bypass line going back into tower tank above pumps check valve. It must be located inside building so it does not freeze in low ambient conditions. Make sure this water line is pitched properly so that water drains back into tower tank properly when tower is shut down.

E. Make sure on process water pump side that there will always be water flow even when all injection molding machines or water cooled chiller is not running (water regulating valves). If there is not some type of continuous water flow, It's strongly recommended to be installed to prevent mechanical seal on pump from burning up and eventually leaking. (Shut off discharge valve before starting any water pumps.)

F. Bump pumps and check rotations and tower fan motor. Change phases for proper rotation; preferably at main terminals or at each motor's contactor (3 phase only). Still make sure on single phase motors. **Slowly open up discharge valves for all pumps.**

G. Make sure all of these checks are done. Then start up tower system and check all operations.

H. Make sure that you make amperage checks on all pump motors only when all water lines are free flowing going to process or to tower. You may have to valve back on supply valve above pump discharge to have motor running at a safe amperage.

I. **Important things**

    a.   Rotation of pumps and fan motors

    b.   Water bleed off line above circulation pumps – check valve that is located inside that leads into tank. Purpose is to drain water from outside tower system so that it does not freeze during low ambient conditions.

    c.   Properly pitched water that leads into top of tank so that all water that is outside will drain back into tower water reservoir tank to prevent it from freezing up outside tower (when they shut down tower system).

    d.   Make sure process pump side has continuous flow at all times so mechanical seal does not fail.

    e.   Proper voltages (check overload settings)

    f.   Final amperage checks on pump motors during maximum water flow usage. Check tower fan motor also.

    g.   Make sure there is a water make up line from city water for evaporation refill. Must have a float valve or an electric level sensor with solenoid valve.

J.   Remember all towers are selected when sold to take into consideration geographic location. All towers should be efficient no matter what ambient, 100% humidity and so on. Remember, towers evaporate no matter what the conditions. Just remember the tower tonnage is based on the ambient and dew point temperatures at the operational location, among other factors.

---

18. CONDEMNING ANY COMPRESSOR OR MOTOR, MAKE THESE CHECKS:

A.   Shut off main power to unit. Manually press contactor for any motor you are checking, including the compressor. First check the proper continuity through just the compressor. Make sure that there is not

---

an open or cross over occurring with the contactor. This is especially important since some higher voltage 3 phase motors will try to run on 2 of the 3 phases of electricity coming to the motor. It does not sound right and can burn up the motor winding very quickly.

B.   Now remove all three lines and the ground directly from the motor itself. Check to ground for any shorts. Also check continuity between each leg. If you do not find any grounds or shorts and the continuity looks okay for the size of the motor, then use an instrument called a megometer. A megometer is an instrument that simulates high voltage to check for grounds and/or shorts. This is the ultimate way of confirming a motor's integrity.

John C. Schaub

Chapter 6

CONVERSION EQUATIONS AND REFERENCES

POWER

1 horsepower = 746 watts

1 horsepower = .746 kilowatts

1 horsepower hr. = 2545 Btu

1 kilowatt hr. = 3412 Btu

1 watt = 3.413 Btu/hr

1 Btu/hour = .293 watts

1 kilowatt = 1.341 horsepower

Power = Current x Voltage (P = I V)

1 Watt is the power from a current of 1 Ampere flowing through 1 Volt.

1 kilowatt-hour is the energy of one kilowatt power flowing for one hour.
   (E = P t).

LIQUID AND PRESSURES

1 atmosphere = 14.7 pounds per square inch absolute (psia)

1 pound per square inch = 2.31 feet head of water

A BTU (British Thermal Unit) is the amount of heat necessary to raise one pound of water by 1 degree Fahrenheit (F).

1 ton of refrigeration = 12,000 Btu per hr

1 gallon of water weighs 8.3 lb

1 liter = .2642 US gallons

1 US quart = .9463 liters

1 US gallon = 3.785 liters

1 inch head of water = 5.20 pounds per square foot

TEMPERATURE

Fahrenheit to Celsius: C = (F-32) * 5/9

Celsius to Fahrenheit: F = (C * 9/5) + 32

John C. Schaub

Bibliography

R.S.E.S Service Manual: Refrigeration and its application.
York Institute of Refrigeration: York Service Manual

About the Book

The **Life of an HVAC/R Technician** contains a detailed explanation of troubleshooting techniques and answers to many questions of how and why systems have failed. This book will save you precious time, money and accelerate your learning curve dramatically. It will include everything from techniques and stories to safety tips and unit sizing.

TESTIMONIALS:

Remarkably detailed... this service manual is especially helpful for first-time service technicians just beginning in an expanding field of refrigeration.

--12 year lead technician Scott Pointon

Schaub's 60 years in the business expands on the decades of changes from belt driven compressors to the age of computerization.

--Dick Weirauch --45 Year service veteran of United Refrigeration

It is about time that someone came out with a handbook that any service technician can easily carry and use on an everyday basis.

--Charles Gardener - 30 year HVAC/R service veteran.

"Thank you for letting me know your view about the energy issues facing our Nation". This quote was written in a letter of appreciation from George W. Bush - President of the United States. (actual letter enclosed)

--George W. Bush - President of the United States

Acknowledgment from the President of the United States George W. Bush, relating to energy savings; written by John C. Schaub.

THE WHITE HOUSE

WASHINGTON

July 25, 2001

Mr. John C. Schaub
President
Schaub Consulting
9 Longhill Court
Medford, New Jersey 08055-9319

Dear Mr. Schaub:

Thank you for letting me know your views about the energy issues facing our Nation.

The past lack of a comprehensive national energy policy has led directly to the energy supply crisis and the high prices Americans face today. In order to prevent high prices and disruptions in the future, we must enact a long-term, comprehensive plan that will encourage conservation, boost our energy supply in an environmentally sound manner, and modernize our energy infrastructure. I have accordingly made energy policy one of the top priorities of my Administration. My National Energy Policy lays out more than 100 recommendations that will light the way to a brighter future by ensuring that energy will be abundant, reliable, cleaner, and more affordable in years to come.

In the short term, my Administration is aggressively removing obstacles to supply, increasing conservation measures, and protecting low-income families from soaring energy costs. My policy will reduce America's dependence on foreign oil and will build stronger relationships with energy producing nations in our own hemisphere. It will also enable our energy supplies to grow while ensuring the highest environmental standards. It promotes the expanded use of clean, efficient technologies like solar energy, automobiles that run on electricity and fuel cells, and power projects that use energy efficiently by simultaneously producing heat and electricity. My policy will modernize our fuel and electricity infrastructure so that we can move energy to where it is needed.

I have great faith in our country's ability to solve energy problems, and my energy policy shows the way. Enclosed is an overview of the policy that I hope is helpful to you. Best wishes.

Sincerely,

George W. Bush

John C. Schaub

About the Author

John Schaub has written articles for many publications such as RSES, Sam's manual, Carrier and York to name a few. John's 60 year career spanned from Kramer Trenton's assembly line in the 40's to working as Worthington's chiller start up specialist for the Eastern United States. During time with Worthington he designed and created the first portable all glass refrigeration system in the world. The collaboration of his years in the business has been a true work in progress. This book was designed and created with the help of his son Rich Schaub, (Superior Images Inc.- professional photography) and his son Jack Schaub – now owner of John's near 40 year service business John C. Schaub Inc. John Schaub has a true passion for his work and an even greater passion to pass on that knowledge to the many interested service technicians around the world.

Education & Background–John C. Schaub, Sr.
York Corporation HVAC/R-graduate 1953
I.C.S. Electrical Engineering–graduate 1968
Member ASHRAE 45 years
Member RSES (CMS) 46 years
President-owner: John C. Schaub, Inc.-30 years
President-owner: Schaub Consulting-11 years
Website: www.chillers.com/schaub.htm
EPA Certification-Universal
National seminar speaker HVAC/R and Chiller Unit Specialist
Writer-HVAC and chiller articles-"The News", RSES

**John Schaub will be traveling throughout the United States performing training seminars and preventative maintenance instruction.

John C. Schaub, Sr.
Phone: 609-859-2138
Southampton, NJ 08088   e-mail: schaubconsulting@comcast.net

Website: www.chillers.com/schaub.htm

Printed in the United States
By Bookmasters